County Council

Libraries, books and more.........

ULL 1 23

ULVERSTON 3 0 MAR 2023		
− 7 MAR 2023	3 0 MAR 2023	
2023		
	0 3 MAY 2023	

Please return/renew this item by the last date due.
Library items may also be renewed by phone on
030 33 33 1234 (24 hours) or via our website

www.cumbria.gov.uk/libraries

Cumbria Libraries

CLIC

Interactive Catalogue

Ask for a CLIC password

Victorian Fashions
for Women

Nellie Hunt sporting the latest summer fashions, taken in Wicks photographic studio, Chelmsford, c1900.

Victorian Fashions for Women

Fiona Kay and Neil R Storey

PEN & SWORD HISTORY

First published in Great Britain in 2022 by
Pen & Sword History
An imprint of
Pen & Sword Books Ltd
Yorkshire – Philadelphia

ISBN 978 1 39900 416 9

Typeset by Mac Style
Printed and bound in the UK by CPI Group (UK) Ltd,
Croydon, CR0 4YY.

Pen & Sword Books Limited incorporates the imprints of Atlas,
Archaeology, Aviation, Discovery, Family History, Fiction, History,
Maritime, Military, Military Classics, Politics, Select, Transport,
True Crime, Air World, Frontline Publishing, Leo Cooper, Remember
When, Seaforth Publishing, The Praetorian Press, Wharncliffe
Local History, Wharncliffe Transport, Wharncliffe True Crime
and White Owl.

For a complete list of Pen & Sword titles please contact

PEN & SWORD BOOKS LIMITED
47 Church Street, Barnsley, South Yorkshire, S70 2AS, England
E-mail: enquiries@pen-and-sword.co.uk
Website: www.pen-and-sword.co.uk

Or

PEN AND SWORD BOOKS
1950 Lawrence Rd, Havertown, PA 19083, USA
E-mail: Uspen-and-sword@casematepublishers.com
Website: www.penandswordbooks.com

*This book is dedicated to our friend Eve,
our very own Queen Victoria.*

Contents

A beautiful bodice with leg-o-mutton sleeves and the high collar characteristic of this period. Her hair is also typically soft and frizzed, c.1894.

Introduction

M ost of us have them, those Victorian portrait photographs mounted on the cards of long gone photographers, depicting people we never knew and probably cannot name. Their names are often not recorded on the card because those who originally owned the photographs knew who the person was in the portraits. Curiously though, if it is a family album, even if we cannot name them, we feel an affinity with the people on the photographs as we look beyond the costumes and hairstyles of the past, and the whiskers of the men, to spot familiar family features.

You also see these old photographs at antique fairs, flea markets and online auctions, old photos of people, often fading but always intriguing, what was their name? What did they do? Where did they live? Such questions captured the imaginations of both authors of this book who have collected and researched these photographs for years. For Neil it was the social history the photographs recorded, for Fiona a fascination with what they were wearing and together, the stories present a fascinating insight into the fashions, times and people of the Victorian era.

Queen Victoria ascended the throne in 1837, her reign lasted sixty-four years and would see Britain reach the apogee of its days of Empire as well as its political and manufacturing powers becoming second to none. The wealth of styles, fashions, arts and literature enjoyed by the British people embodied this and reflected so much of the affluence of the times. The Victorian age can be divided into three distinct periods beginning with the Early Victorian or Romantic Era (c.1837–1861), Middle Victorian or Grand Era (c.1861–1885) and the Late Victorian or Aesthetic Era (c.1885–1901).

The period of Queen Victoria's reign was also a time of discovery and invention, not just in Britain but throughout the world. It saw the expansion of railways, steam-driven road transport, the arrival of electricity, indoor plumbing and saw the long-needed improvement of

Lady's Pictoral, July 1897.

sanitation take place, especially in urban areas. There was the invention of the telephone, the advent of photography and even moving pictures.

For the world of fashion, the industrial revolution of the late eighteenth and early nineteenth centuries had created water and steam-driven specialist machinery for textile manufacture. Mills were built that were rapidly capable of the mass production of millions of yards of textiles, and factories developed production lines with some machine processes such as stitching for boots and shoes for both the home and export market. New and increasingly powerful steam ships, instead of the old tall-masted traders, saw huge quantities of raw materials imported and British-made goods exported all over the world. The wealth rolled in, tragically there were still those suffering terrible poverty and the working conditions, especially in relation to safety, took a long while to improve, but there was more wealth being enjoyed by more people from a wider strata of British society than ever before.

Visible signs of wealth and prosperity were important. Those who owned the big businesses and factories had their big houses, servants, carriages, expensive jewellery and fashionable clothes. The wealth enjoyed by more people during the nineteenth century saw the 'middling sort', who had really begun to emerge in the eighteenth century, become more defined as a middle class. They had their own projections of affluence, such as owning their own home and decorating it in styles that echoed the wealthier classes, made more affordable because they were mass produced through modern industrial processes.

Colourful decorative ceramics such as the Staffordshire pottery 'flatbacks' and pairs of spaniel dogs decorated many a mantle shelf in early Victorian households. As more people enjoyed the benefit of earning more money the demand for 'something more' hastened the potteries to produce what to modern eyes might appear as quite gaudy vases, candle holders and spill holders with transfer printed images of painted flowers, birds, animals and country idylls, but they brought feature and colour to rooms of rich coloured drapery and dark furniture.

Expensive hand-painted plates and tiles were created on cheaper transfer-printed pottery, especially in the chinoiserie Willow pattern, that would be a well-loved staple design for dinner services produced by just about every British pottery manufacturer well into the twentieth century. Electroplated nickel silver (EPNS) saw cheap cutlery and cruet sets made in fine designs (previously only made in hallmarked silver) adorn many a table, along with fancy cut glassware, decorative coloured lamps and spelter figurines painted to look like bronze that all helped achieve the desired styles and ambience of the living spaces of the middle class. Working-class households were not going to be left out either, eating their day-to-day meals in the kitchen, many took great pride in maintaining a 'front room' or parlour where family and friends would only gather for special occasions.

More people than ever could enjoy fashionable clothes too as mass production brought down the cost of fabric and aniline dyes (discovered by chance in 1856 by British chemist William Perkin in his basic home laboratory as he tried to synthesise quinine for the treatment of malaria) were developed to enable clothes to be created in a wonderful array of colours and printed fabric designs. By 1860 there were over 2,600 cotton mills in Lancashire alone, employing in excess of 440,000 employees producing half the world's spun and woven cotton, and still producing 8 billion yards of cloth a year in 1900.

The dissemination of fashion and the details of the latest styles of the season had been conveyed through printed literature since the late eighteenth century by periodicals containing hand-coloured fashion plates. Among the earliest were *Gallery of Fashion*, first published by Nicolaus Heideloff in 1794, that ran for nearly ten years. Then the *Records of Fashion and Court Elegance* published 1807–1809 described in its day as 'for the edification of the ladies … with much propriety addressed to the female nobility',[1] it also included reviews of music and theatre

Lady's Pictorial, Christmas 1891.

Advert for W.H. Barlow, Leeds, hatter, clothier and waterproofer, 1852.

performances, a 'Journal of Polite Intelligence', 'Courtley Events' and 'Private Assemblages', in other words the most genteel of gossip columns.

Records of Fashion was the first women's fashion magazine to be published under the direction of a woman, a certain Mrs Fiske, a notable milliner and dressmaker of her day who owned a shop on New Bond Street at the heart of London's West End, the haunt of the most fashionable young ladies and gentlemen of the day.

In the lineage of women's fashion magazines the mantle of doyen and arbiter of taste and style would pass in turn to Mrs Mary Ann Bell (née Millard), owner of The Fashionable Millinery and Dress Rooms on King Street, Covent Garden, fashion editor of *La Belle Assemblée or Bell's Court and Fashionable Magazine addressed particularly to Ladies*, from its first edition in 1806.

Its publisher was John Bell (1745–1841), an innovative printer who came to prominence among the reading public for producing some of the first affordable, illustrated printed books. His son John Brown Bell

(1779–1855) had married Mary Ann in 1806 and it seems they were struck with the novel idea of Mary not only having a fashionable dress shop with a fresh display of costumes on the first day of every month, but to have a magazine that would, in addition to theatrical reviews, short stories and a smattering of genteel gossip, both promote and illustrate these garments under the guise of editorial comment. Thus began a new dynasty in fashion publishing.

Bell sold *La Belle Assemblée* in 1821 but would return to the fashion scene again with a new magazine originally entitled *World of Fashion and Continental Feuilletons* with Mary Ann Bell as director. Mary was now the proud owner of new shop premises entitled Magazin des Modes on Cleveland Road, opposite St James's Palace, offering millinery, dresses and head-dresses 'prepared in Paris for Mrs Bell'. She also proudly advertised that she 'exclusively' took delivery of 'every foreign novelty' twice a week. *World of Fashion* ran from 1824 to 1851.[2] After the death of his father, John Browne Bell took over at the helm of their printing offices at 299, Strand, London.

In 1850, *World of Fashion* became the first fashion magazine to include a free paper pattern inside. The pattern would enable the lady in possession of it to make her own dress or more likely, considering the class the magazine was aimed at, she could take it to her own seamstress to have a dress made in the very latest style of those being worn in fashionable London.

The early fashion magazines had been aimed at the women of noble and wealthy families. They were prohibitively expensive for most women who did not have the benefit of a large income or allowance. In 1844 *Townsend's Selection of Parisian Costumes* cost 1shilling and in 1850 a copy of *The World of Fashion* also cost 1 shilling, the equivalent of a day's pay for a skilled man at that time, but it would not stay that way forever.

The notion of a steam-driven printing press had been around for decades but it was only in 1843 the steam-powered rotary press was invented in the United States by Richard M. Hoe. Hoe's invention enabled millions of pages of printed text to be produced in a single day and, combined with development of the railways, cheap, mass-circulation newspapers and magazines began appearing across America, continental Europe and Britain like never before.

The next generation of women's fashion magazines developed as more people had more money, because there were more newspapers, periodicals

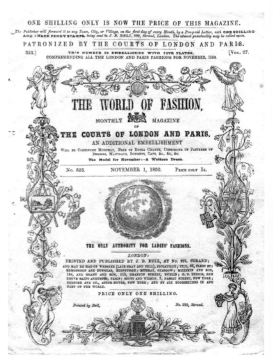

The cover of Townsend's Monthly Selection of
Parisian Costumes, *June 1844.*

The World of Fashion, Monthly magazine of
the Courts of London and Paris, *November 1,
1850.*

and magazines available more and more people were learning to read
and because newspapers offered reportage and stories aimed at female
readers, including the latest fashions for women; there was plenty for
them to read about.

Samuel Orchart Beeton, the publisher who had enjoyed great success
as the first British publisher of *Uncle Tom's Cabin*, was determined to
build on his success by launching not one, but two magazines aimed
specifically at two very different readerships in 1852. Both magazines
would contain engaging readers' letters and popular stories typical of
their time, blended with features offering practical instruction and useful
knowledge. Both magazines would become household names, one would
be *Boy's Own Magazine* and the other *The Englishwoman's Domestic
Magazine*, in which Samuel's wife Isabella would write supplements on
fashion and domestic management between 1859 and 1861. So popular
were these that they became a work in their own right as *Mrs Beeton's Book
of Household Management* first published in 1861.

Priced at just 2d it was the first cheap magazine for young women of the middle class and it soon was claiming a circulation of 50,000 copies for each edition. Every magazine came with a free dress pattern, making *Englishwoman's Domestic* the first magazine to supply the latest fashionable dress patterns to a mass audience. As the 1850s rolled into a new decade and the middle classes continued to expand and become even more affluent, the Beetons continued to appeal to this market by giving *Englishwoman's Domestic* a greater emphasis to its most popular elements of fiction stories and fashion.

Throughout the 1860s mechanical sewing machines were becoming far more affordable and were starting to appear in many middle-class homes and very soon even a housemaid on her day off could wear a similar outfit to that worn by her mistress, the only difference being the quality of the fabric. Industrialisation made production of fabrics and dress trimmings cheaper, so the crinoline was adopted by all levels of society. The 1870s were a decade of over abundant trimmings which would have been prohibitively expensive to buy when made by hand and hugely time consuming to sew on without a sewing machine. The use of aniline dyes brought a never-before seen vibrancy, some say vulgarity, to the colours worn. That said, the Women's Suffrage movement was garnering support and found a national voice in the National Society for Women's Suffrage, more women than ever wanted to read about it and felt empowered to make the dresses in the styles and colours *they* wanted to wear.

To get a better idea of the the changing fashions actually being worn by women at this time we can learn a great deal from the photographs taken over that period, this was after all the first era to be documented by photographers, and they show what was actually worn, not what the fashion journals thought should be worn. But it should be remembered that having your photograph taken was a special occasion, it was something you would save up for, you would want to look your best and would wear your best clothes, or even borrow garments or accessories from friends to complete the look.

In some photographs skirts show creases or fold marks in them. This was deemed as something of a status symbol, particularly on the Continent, as it implied a never-before worn garment purchased especially for the photograph. To see a smile on a photograph was also unusual, this has led to suggestions that there were no smiles because they had to sit still for minutes on end as the photographic image was exposed. This may have been the case in very early photographs, such as daguerreotypes, where a neck brace was used by some photographers to ensure their sitters kept still, but as technology advanced exposure times soon came down to around a minute. However, it was a process that was prohibitively expensive for most people, a single Daguerrotype cost between 7 and 30 shillings each. Even at the lower end of the market it would equate to a

Four sisters in identical dresses, c1872.

week's wages for a skilled man at that time. Photography continued to advance and the development of the wet collodion process with glass negatives in 1851 enabled a high-quality image to be captured in seconds of exposure rather than minutes. These images would be printed from the negative onto photographic paper mounted on stiff card that usually bore the details of the photographer accompanied with the motto: 'additional copies can be obtained'.

The process cost a lot less and soon there were photographers setting up their studios in cities and towns across the country. Prices for customers did come down but even in the 1890s the best London studios were still commanding three guineas a portrait, although the cheaper 'carte de visite' photographers were down to 2s 6d a dozen. With the advent of the carte de visite in the early 1850s a mania for collecting them emerged soon after that became a phenomena known as cartomania. Having obtained the twelve prints of your photographic portrait as 4½ × 2½ inches (11.4 × 6.3 cm) carte de visites from your photographer, you could then swap and share them with friends and family. Many photographers would also sell copies of the notable personalities who had sat for them, or copy photographs by other studios of the royal family, actors and actresses,

CHAUSSURES FRANCAISES.
Smallest appearance to the foot and greatest comfort.

Monsieur M. ARMAND
(Late Manager, Paris Boot Co., Regent Street),

Has the honour to inform his numerous Lady Patrons that he is no
longer connected with the above firm, and begs to call
Special attention to his new address,
AS FOLLOWS:

7, CRANBOURNE ST., LONDON, W.C.
New Illustrated Price List Free on application.

Gaiety Theatre programme, 1881.

leading politicians, infamous criminals, society beauties and other famous dignitaries. Swapping became a popular pursuit, much in the way way that more recent generations have swapped collectors' cards of film stars, football players or cartoon characters, and special albums with pages to slot the photographs into were produced.

So why did most sitters still not smile? This was purely because the photograph was looked on as a new painted portrait, where you would have to hold a pose for hours and a smile was seldom seen. Only the wealthy could afford to have their portrait painted, photographs were ultimately available to the masses, but having your photographic portrait taken was not cheap and remained a serious business. The assumption also lingers, because there were so many serious faces on these photographs, that our Victorian ancestors were a dour people, but over recent years photographs, especially flick books of multiple photographs that appear to show the sitters moving when you thumb through the pages at speed, show our ancestors smiling and laughing and even getting the giggles as they try to keep a straight face for the photographer. They really were not the sullen lot we thought they were after all. Well, not all of them.

Carte de Visites and their larger version, the Cabinet Card, usually measuring 6½ × 4¼ inches, present a fascinating photographic record of the Victorians and what they wore. They can also lead to the bemusement of those who inherit these albums and are unaware of the cartomania phenomena, as to the family intrigues and secrets that led to Prime Minister Gladstone's photograph appearing on the same page as the photograph of great-great-granny, and further on in the book a little research reveals one of the women pictured is not another previously unknown great aunt, but the infamous Victorian suspected poisoner

Bullimore & Son, draper stores, North Walsham, Norfolk, c.1895.

Adelaide Bartlett. For costume historians however, these photographs are a priceless record of how we used to look.

Women's fashions changed quite rapidly and distinctly during the Victorian era, once you know what to look for it becomes quite easy to pinpoint the styles of an outfit to a decade and even date it to within a handful of years. Tragically, black and white photographs, despite the best efforts of some photographers to occasionally tint them, give no idea of the cornucopia of fabric prints and colours achieved during the reign of Queen Victoria. Day to day, like most of our clothes down the centuries, the clothes of most people would not have been too outlandish in their colours but dresses and their accessories for special occasions would have been striking.

Colours and print patterns may have enjoyed many shades and designs, but before synthetics the fabrics themselves remained fairly constant, being variations of silk, wool, cotton, linen and velvet, although these variations are known by a multitude of names, many of which are now obsolete. The Victorian era saw some of the best-known extremes of fashion, from crinoline cages to tight-laced corsets, it also saw movements against these fashions but as the *Glasgow Herald* sagely pointed out: 'the feud between reason and fashion is an ancient one'.[3]

This book does not aim to be a comprehensive, in-depth study of Victorian fashions and clothing. Nor does it detail the varying degrees of formality around what was required to be worn at what time of day over the decades. Suffice to say this was rather complicated at times for the middle and upper classes. Not only was there 'undress' (informal, high-necked, long-sleeved), 'half dress' (showing a little more) and 'full dress' (plunging necklines and bare arms), but within these there were also rules for at home in the morning, afternoon, evening, carriage, promenades, walking, visiting, receptions, the theatre, dinner parties, balls, dances and so on. A lady on a four-day visit could need up to sixteen outfits as she was not expected to wear the same one twice. It must have been tiresome indeed having to change outfits so often. Nor is the book aimed at studying the high-end market, the likes of Charles Frederick Worth, considered the father of Haute Couture and credited, among other things, as the first designer to use live mannequins to display his designs. Hopefully, what it will provide is an insight and understanding of the changes in women's fashion throughout the Victorian era and encourage further reading, research and enjoyment of this fascinating and multi-layered subject which we warmly commend to you.

Fiona Kay and Neil Storey

Queen Victoria and Prince Albert on their wedding day in 1840, notice the yards of Honiton lace on her dress.

Chapter 1

1840s

At 6am on the 20 June 1837, 18-year-old Alexandrina Victoria was woken to be told that she was now Queen of the United Kingdom of Great Britain and Ireland. As a wealthy, young, fashionable woman, Victoria would have enjoyed the exaggerated fashions of the early years of the 1830s when sleeves were inflated until they became large, sloping gigot sleeves, the shoulder width being further emphasised by wide necklines, white pelerines and tippets resting on the sleeves.

The wide emphasis on the upper part of the body was balanced out by the conical skirt, this along with the wide shoulders made the corseted low, narrow waist look even smaller. Hair was dressed in elaborate curls, loops and knots sticking out from both the sides and top of the head. During the second half of the 1830s the exaggerated fashions were beginning to diminish. The bodice starts to become tighter, longer and more pointed at the waistline, the skirt widens, the shoulder-line drops, and is set much lower on the arm, and the huge balloon-like sleeves deflate.

The *Ladies Pocket Magazine* declared:

The principle change is expected to be in the sleeves. Some have been already introduced, made quite tight to the arm, but ornamented with ruches in such a manner as did not at all add to their volume. We have seen also some others decorated with puffs placed in a spiral direction, and so small as to take off but little of the tightness of the sleeve.[1]

The hair also subsided, losing both height and width, to be arranged flat against the head with loops or ringlets over the ears. Victoria's accession coincided with a period of Romanticism, with idealised concepts of love and valour which, with a tendency towards sentiment and nostalgia, embodied the idea of modest gentility in a woman.

The Romantic Era

The first years of Victoria's reign, from 1837–1861, are known as the Romantic Era. It was a period when Britain was steadily moving from an agricultural country to a modern industrialised nation and its leading poets, writers and artists embraced Romanticism, harking back to an imagined and glorified past of knights, chivalry, heroic deeds, maidens and castles in the Britain that was then Albion, or the Avalon of King Arthur as epitomised in Mallory's *Le Morte de Arthur*, which proved a regular inspiration for authors of the Romantic period. With this lost England of the past that never was, there was entwined the inspiration of nature, pure and unsullied by industrialisation. This was, as William Blake would so eloquently phrase it in his preface to his epic *Milton: A Poem in Two Books* (1808), the 'green and pleasant land' where he pondered whether the countenance divine did shine upon our clouded hills and if Jerusalem was 'builded here among these dark Satanic Mills'.

Townsend's Monthly Selection of Parisian Costumes, June 1844.

The works of the 'Romantic' authors such as William Wordsworth, John Keats, Lord Byron, Percy Bysshe Shelly, Walter Scott and Samuel Taylor Coleridge were extremely popular among the educated middle and upper classes and the vogue for romanticised ideas and imagery of a medieval England resulted in a craze for medieval costume balls.

The Earl of Eglinton took the theme to a new level when he staged a Tournament in 1839. Planned to run over three days in late August at Eglinton Castle in North Ayrshire, the earl spent over twelve months and upwards of £20,000 organising it, the equivalent of £2,211,000 today (2022). Those who wanted to joust trained as knights, medieval encampments emblazoned with banners and crests were built along with viewing stands to seat hundreds, there were also to be large tents to hold a banquet and ball. The earl expected 4,000 spectators; in the end it is estimated around 100,000 people turned up. *The World of Fashion* reported:

> The sports are to occupy 3 days. The procession to the lists will leave Eglinton Castle about the noon of each day, and will comprise the knights, their esquires and retainers, the king of the list, and the lord of the tournament, the queen of beauty and the other principal personages who will figure this revival of the glories of other days.[2]

Spectators were encouraged to wear medieval costume, and many arrived appropriately attired as reported by *The Globe*:

> The Earl of Eglington has intimated a wish that all who can appear in any costume of the middle ages will do so; and it is a matter of astonishment to remark how tastefully the ancient dress is imitated.[3]

The article then proceeds to describe some of the costumes worn by participants including that of Lady Seymour, 'The Queen of Beauty':

> Dressed in a robe of violet, with the Seymour crest embroidered in silver on blue velvet, the gorget or upper part of the bodice ornamented by a mass of precious stones and gold; a cloak of cerise velvet trimmed with gold and ermine; headdress, a cap covering part of the neck, barred with gold, each bar being ornamented with a row

of pearls; and riding on a horse superbly caparisoned; a draperied canopy borne over her by attendants in costumes, attended by four petit pages in costly costumes.[4]

All was set for the most spectacular event. Unfortunately, as the parade was due to set off, the great British weather did what it can do at times and the heavens opened in a sudden, violent rainstorm. The Queen of Beauty was quickly ushered into a carriage to be driven to the arena as the rest of the parade dutifully carried on, arriving thoroughly waterlogged. The jousting field rapidly became a quagmire making it difficult to joust, the grandstand roofs leaked and the banqueting tents became so waterlogged that the banquet and ball were cancelled and the audience started leaving in droves:

> Hundreds of spectators hurried away as fast as their legs could carry them; splashing themselves and their neighbours in the most woeful manner as they trode [*sic*] through the universal puddle, into which the ground had been converted by the torrents. Never in my life did I witness such an exhibition. There was something irresistibly comic in the distress of the flying multitude. Up went many scores of fine silk dresses, which the fair wearers were all solicited to shield from damage; and off came hundreds of pairs of shoes and stockings, from the feet of both men and women, young and old, which were safely stowed away in baskets or in great coat pockets.[5]

It was a disastrous start to the event; day two was cancelled outright but it was agreed to hold a second joust on the third and final day. Thankfully, the weather was kinder, crowds gathered again, although in fewer numbers, the procession took place as did the jousting. Even the formal ball and banquet went ahead, the latter with 2,000 guests, most in medieval costume. However, heavy rain returned towards the end of the ball and it was agreed to end the event. The Eglinton Tournament was intended to be one of the most elaborate events in this era of Romanticism; Doulton and Ridgway potteries would even make commemorative jugs in its honour, it but the lasting legacy of the Eglington Tournament was that it had been 'the most splendid folly of the age'.[6]

The romanticising of all things medieval was carried on by the Pre-Raphaelite Brotherhood, founded in 1848 by a group of painters and art critics, including Dante Gabriel Rosetti and John Everett Millais. Their aim was to bring all art back to nature and free it from what they perceived to be inhibiting 'academic conventions'. The artists involved admired the natural, free look of female dress in medieval art with its flowing gowns, natural waists and wide sleeves.

The models for their paintings were dressed to mimic these medieval styles in loose fitting, relatively plain, long, flowing gowns, often with puffed sleeves in muted, natural colours. It became known as Artistic Dress and soon both the models and artists' wives and sisters adopted the look for everyday wear, but the look remained limited to bohemian and artistic circles, to those who rejected the social norms. It was an extreme contrast to contemporary fashion for clothing that, as they saw it, distorted nature. Their emphasis was on natural colour and shape, with a belief that garments should be hand-made from quality materials, a reaction to the increasing mechanisation of the Victorian age. Materials like silk and velvet in colours such as sage green and terracotta were preferred, decoration was limited to natural motifs such as embroidered flowers.

The Royal Wedding

The first year of the new decade began in elaborate style with the wedding of Queen Victoria to Prince Albert of Saxe-Coburg and Gotha on 10 February 1840. This was to be the first royal wedding that could really be called a public event, with the young queen travelling in a procession of carriages along cheering crowded streets, from Buckingham Palace to the Royal Chapel of St James's Palace. The queen's perceived innocence, obvious love for her husband-to-be and her refusals to wear the crimson velvet robes of state fitted perfectly with the Romanticised notions of love and individuality of the time.

Instead, she opted for a white gown probably made by Her Majesty's dressmaker Mrs Mary Bettans. It was off the shoulder with elbow-length gathered sleeves, deep lace flounces at the neck and sleeves and a bodice with a deep V-shape at the waistline, the skirt was floor-length and very full, containing seven widths of fabric measuring 139 inches (3.5m) in circumference. The satin train over six yards (5.5m) long and was carried by twelve attendants, her veil and the flounce in her dress were of matching lace and her slippers matched the colour of the dress. Her outfit was described in detail in a number of newspapers:

Her Majesty the Queen wore on her head a wreath of orange blossom and a veil of Honiton lace, with a necklace and earrings of diamonds. Her Majesty's dress was of white satin, with a deep trimming of Honiton lace, in design similar to that of the veil. The body and sleeves were richly trimmed with the same material to correspond. The train was of white satin, and was also lined with white satin, trimmed with orange blossom (white). The cost of the lace of the lace on the Queens dress was £1,000. The satin was of pure white. Her majesty wore an armlet having the motto of the Order of the garter, 'Honi soit qui mal y pense,' inscribed, and also wore the star of the order. The lace which formed the flounce of the dress measures four yards and is three-quarters of a yard in depth.[7]

The orange blossom was a symbol of fertility and rather than a tiara, Victoria wore a wreath made of the delicate flower over her veil, the latter measuring four yards (3.5m) long and three-quarters of a yard (just over half a metre) wide. Her jewellery consisted of diamond necklace, earrings given to her by the Sultan of Turkey, and a sapphire cluster brooch recently given to her by Albert.

Her gown was made from purely British materials, purposefully patronising industries that were in decline. The silk fabric for the dress was woven in Spitalfields, East London, and despite the fact that Brussels lace was all the rage, the order was placed with Jane Bidney of Middlesex who had received the queen's first Royal Appointment to a maker of Honiton lace in 1837. Miss Bidney was a native of Beer in Devon, an area famous for its handmade lace, an industry that was suffering badly from the development of mass-produced machine lace. Victoria commissioned about 200 lace workers local to Beer for the project, bringing them nine months of work making lace using traditional designs at a reported cost of £1,000, although this cannot be confirmed. The overall design used for the veil and dress trim were destroyed once the work was completed, ensuring that it would remain unique. The young queen was so pleased with the result that Jane Bidney was invited to attend the wedding and her workers were sent money to hold a celebration on the day. The lace flounce alone measured 4 yards and is three-quarters of a yard in depth (3.5m × 0.69m), this and her veil became some of Victoria's most treasures possessions and she continued to wear them on special occasions throughout her life. For eight of her nine children she had the lace mounted onto the dresses she wore to their christenings, the only exception was her first-born son, and heir to the throne, Albert Edward, for whom she wore her Garter robes. It was used again on dresses she wore for the marriages of her eldest daughter, Victoria, and her youngest son, Leopold; her youngest daughter, Beatrice, was permitted to wear it as part of her wedding gown. Victoria also wore the lace to the wedding of her grandson, George (the future George V), and for her Diamond Jubilee official photographs in 1897. The lace is still in storage but is now far too fragile to be moved. As to her Honiton lace veil, Victoria was buried with this covering her face.

Although Queen Victoria is often credited with being the originator of the white wedding dress, this is not really the case. What can be said is that she made it a more popular choice. Her wedding was, unusually for royalty at that time, quite a public affair; she was seen by thousands, the procession, dress and ceremony were reported in many newspapers and the dress Victoria chose was, for a royal wedding dress, relatively simple, making it easy to imitate. So while Victoria didn't start the 'tradition', she went a long way to making it the symbol for innocence and romance that it became.

The 1840s' Look

Historically, Paris has always taken the lead in European fashion and the Royal courts were a huge influence on the fashions of the well-to-do at this time, the very wealthiest travelling to the city to buy the latest designs. Fashion magazines were read voraciously among the literate who could afford to spend their money on them. The *World of Fashion Monthly Magazine of the Courts of London and Paris* was the arbiter of the latest styles of the season. It had the largest circulation of any such magazine of its day with sales averaging between 3,000–4,000 copies a month, selling to the nobility and gentry throughout Britain, the East and West Indies and America.

Not only did it have beautifully hand-coloured fashion plates, there were also detailed descriptions of the illustrated gowns pointing out their details, accoutrements and accessories. Extracts from *World of Fashion* were also republished in both local and national newspapers, most of which had regular columns on fashion, thus allowing those not so well off to keep up with the latest trends. Paris was the city that influenced London when it came to fashion; where Paris went, London generally followed not too long after. In 1848, however, the revolution in France brought a temporary halt to this; England lost its French inspiration and the evolution of fashion slowed.

The Last & Newest Fashions. 1840. Morning & Evening Dresses. [4]

The World of Fashion, Monthly magazine of the Courts of London and Paris, Illustrates morning and evening dresses in the latest styles, 1 March 1840.

The silhouette of the early 1840s was still very much along the lines of that of the late 1830s, but the overall look started to become much simpler. With fabrics such as silk being expensive it was not unknown for older clothes to be completely taken apart, sent to a dyers and remodelled into a newer, more current style. At the start of Victoria's reign there was a brief revival of eighteenth-century brocaded floral silks, which led to many family heirlooms being unpicked so that the fabric could be reused. Industrial advances in the spinning, weaving, printing and general manufacture of cotton fabrics in the eighteenth century produced reasonably priced patterned fabrics. This and the ever-growing industrialisation of lace and embroidery production began to bring up-to-date fashions within reach of more people

The 1840s bodice became longer and narrower, coming to a deep point at the front, well below the waist, which emphasised the expanding skirt. By now, the side seams and darts were boned and often highlighted with piping in the same material as the dress, or a similar coloured fabric. As well as providing a subtle decoration, this helped stiffen seams and give the dress a greater definition. Flat pleats converging from shoulder to waist ran down the bodice front in a deep V. These were known as 'revers de pelerine', and were a visual way of drawing the eye down and helping to create the illusion of a narrow waist. Alternatively, the pleats could be more fan shaped, producing a similar effect. Necklines were rounded and moderately high for daywear, often with a white collar, or berthe, of lace, muslin, or cambric, with matching under sleeves; these continued until about 1844 when higher necklines became popular, staying in fashion for the next twenty years or so. Until 1846, when the separate skirt and bodice made an appearance, the dress was one piece, fastening at the back with either hooks and eyelet holes or lacings. The new bodice was front-fastening, fitted to the waist and had a 'basque', or bodice extension below the waist.

In the mid-1830s sleeves became tighter at the top and bottom and pleated, ruched or gathered round the elbow, but by the early 1840s long narrowing sleeves had replaced them. Occasionally these had a 'mancheron', or ornamental trimming, on the upper part of the sleeve. Shoulders had developed a distinct slope by mid-century and sleeves were becoming tighter; being set below the shoulder, they restricted arm movement, making it difficult to raise the arm much above a right angle.

By the end of the decade, sleeves started to widen at the cuff and at the same time the bodice waist began to shorten and lose its point. In the years before modern deodorant, perspiration was a problem and in the later 1830s and 40s 'dress preservers' became popular. Made of rubber or chamois leather they would be stitched into the dress under the arms.

From 1841 a new way of pleating – gauging – allowed more material to be gathered at the pointed waistline,

> by gauging it round the top as far as the points of the hips; by this means that excessive fullness which would be otherwise disposed in gathers or plaits, is formed exactly to the shape, but on the other hand, this method lengthens the waist excessively, and gives an air of stiffness to the figure, so what is gained in one way, is, perhaps, lost in another.[8]

The gauging pleats were deeper at the centre back where there was the most material. Skirts were now just above the ground and cut from a simple rectangle of fabric, the result was that the skirt became more dome shaped, sticking out abruptly from the waist, and measuring up to four to five yards (3.5 to 4.5m) around the hem. In skirts of heavy materials the bell shape could be aided by a padding of wool between dress and lining round the hips to the back. The *Leeds Intelligencer* issued a warning about the width of the skirt stating: 'the breadth should always be modified to that of the figure, though it should never be so scanty as to prevent the plaits from falling in broad and graceful folds.'[9]

The fashion for gauging lasted for about five years before flat pleating started to replace it. Consequently the padding round the waist was no longer needed; the hemline also rose slightly and a frill around the bottom of the skirt began to appear.

From around 1843 the use of one or two deep flounces on the skirt increased, these were often scalloped and pinked around the edges, hidden under the top flounce, at the waist, you could often find a small watch pocket. The 'pyramid-style' design became popular with horizontal lines of trimming round the skirt becoming narrower as they neared the waist, rows of decorative buttons were also seen. The type of fabric of which the skirt was made would often dictate the type of decoration. Very light materials that could not support embellishments would have either multiple flounces or two larger ones, with the upper one much shorter than the lower. Silk skirts were either plain or had scalloped flounces decorated with ruched ribbon, fringing or bouillon. Plaids would have their flounces cut on the bias and heavy materials had trimmings of passementerie, gimp, buttons, velvet and tassels.

Depending on the weight of the fabric used skirts were lined with cotton Silesia or muslin, and heavier winter skirts often had a lining of flannel. The fabric could be plain or patterned, primary

Cabinet of Fashion, c1848.

colours were not fashionable, but muted secondary such as shades of grey, green and pink were popular. Fabrics such as silks, cottons, tarlatan, velvets, light wools and wool mixes predominated. Industrial advances meant that both fabric-printing and lace-making processes were not only improving the quality of goods available but also reducing costs, making them available to more than just the wealthy.

Colours and styles of fashions can be influenced by many factors and vagaries, but occasionally a far darker event will influence the disregarding of a style or material because of its association with the likes of sickness, disease, death or murder. A prime example occurred in the last year of the decade, when husband and wife Frederick and Maria Manning were found guilty of having murdered Maria's former lover, Patrick O'Connor. A crime made even more notorious because the pair had buried O'Connor's body under their kitchen floor. The Mannings, perpetrators of what the press and chap books dubbed 'The Bermondsey Horror', were hanged on the roof Horsemonger Lane Gaol in front of a huge crowd on 13 November 1849. Maria Manning wore a black satin dress for her own hanging and consequently the material was shunned by English women for years afterwards. Maria was dubbed 'the woman who murdered black satin'.

Foundation Garments

By 1837 what had previously been ankle-length skirts were back to ground length and the expanding skirt needed to be supported by several cotton petticoats, starched and stiffened round the hem with rows of cording as well as a stout linen petticoat stiffened with horsehair – the original crinoline. The name itself is derived from the French words 'crin' for horsehair, and 'lin' for the linen thread with which it was woven.

The number of petticoats worn would depend on the season but could be as many as six or seven, with only the outer one showing much in the way of decoration. Scarlet flannel became popular as it was believed that it would ward off chills, rheumatism and the flu. The *Handbook of the Toilette* advises that 'flannel petticoats, and drawers are of incalculable advantage to women, preventing many of the disorders and indispositions to which British females are subject.'[10]

Being next to the skin, white undergarments were washed regularly and the starching of petticoats was a very necessary activity if they were to hold the skirt out to the required shape. Starching would be carried out at home on laundry day. Over the counter starches were available and easy to use. Glenfield Patent Double Refined Powder Starch was very well advertised in the 1840s and included testimonials from the likes of the Lady Mayoress of London and the 'Laundress of the Marchioness of Breadalbane', who said she found 'the quality superior to any I have ever tried. For giving a transparent, clear, elastic finish to laces, linens, &c., it cannot be surpassed.'[11] At least, that is what was quoted in their advertising.

The *Handbook of the Toilette* also advises that 'the drawers of ladies may be made of flannel, angola, calico or even cotton stocking web; they should reach down the leg as far as it is possible to make them without their being seen.'[12]

Despite being mentioned in the handbook and other guides, not every women was wearing drawers, or as they are sometimes called, 'pantalettes', the sheer weight of petticoats and skirt prevented any accidental flashing of the legs and the layers provided warmth. Those that were worn were single legged, attached to a drawstring waistband and open along the crotch seam. Along with the drawers there would be a cotton chemise, short-sleeved, around mid-calf-length and yoked. In the late 1840s and into the 1850s a flap on the front and back at the neck was added which would fold down over the corset to ensure the top would not show above the dress.

Over the chemise and drawers was the corset of cotton twill or coutil, which were usually white or drab in colour. In the 1840s the shaping was achieved using gores, giving rounded cup-shaped bust sections and shaping over the hips. They laced at the back with a single lace, in a spiral pattern from top to bottom, making it impossible to put the corset on without help. At the front there was a busk (a flat length of whalebone, wood or steel) inserted in a channel down the centre to smooth out the front of the dress. The stays extended, as the *Handbook of the Toilette* explains,

> not only over the bosom but also over the abdomen and back down to the hips; besides being so thickly garnished with whalebone, to say nothing of an immense wooden, metal or whalebone busk passing in front from the top of the stays to the bottom[13]

All of which combined to give the torso a somewhat rigid appearance.

Cording or strips of whalebone were used to give the corset more structure, the latter moulding to the shape of the wearer with body heat. Shoulder straps were still worn into the 1840s and for those ladies who felt their natural bust was not big enough they could also buy 'bust improvers' to pad out the corset, *Handbook of the Toilette* talks of 'lemon bosoms and many other means of creating fictitious charms and improving the work of nature'.[14]

Accessories

Outer garments had to accommodate the ever-expanding skirt, and in milder weather large shawls were very fashionable and correct management of a shawl was seen as a sign of gentility; the *Leeds Intelligencer* sung its virtues:

> What is it that, in an instant, converts the indoor dress into a suitable costume for the promenade? The Shawl. What is it which gives a height and nobleness to the back of the figure that no other adjunct of the toilette imparts? The well-arranged Shawl.[15]

Shawls were large and often square, worn folded diagonally to create a triangle. Lightweight ones would be of lace, silk, muslin and organdie, heavier ones of velvet and wool. But those held in highest regard were made in the vale of Kashmir in north west India. Britain took some of its fashion influences from places other than Paris, the *Bristol Mercury* commented:

> Certain it is that Fashion, having exhausted the resources of Europe, finding no shadow of taste in America, and turning away with a blush from African modes, has at length commenced her researches, and exercised her powers of imitation upon Asia.[16]

Cashmere shawls were highly decorated with a teardrop pattern that has come to be known as Paisley, after the Scottish town, one of a number of shawl producers in Britain, but its original name was 'boteh' and it was inspired by the Oriental territories that bordered Kashmir. Woven from the fine underbelly fleece of Tibetan goats, the shawls were expensive and renowned for their softness. British and French manufacturers tried to reproduce the soft feel of cashmere, even attempting to breed Tibetan goats in Britain, but generally without much success.

Norwich had earned a name for itself for the manufacture of quality shawls since the 1790s and a viable alternative to cashmere was created in the city by Alderman John Harvey at his manufactory on Colegate. Joined in 1792 by Mr P.J. Knights, they commenced making the shawls woven in wool on a silk warp, the outline of the pattern being printed, while the flower was embroidered with needles by hand, a process that was greatly speeded up by the introduction to the city of Jacquard looms from the 1830s.

Norwich shawls were soft, warm, and strong. The city produced the most beautiful square fringed shawls decorated with 'boteh' of all sizes. They were measured in quarter yards, e.g. ⁵⁄₄ or 45 inches, ⁶⁄₄ or 54 inches wide, and were often square. Large shawls could measure 6ft (2m) square, filled with 'boteh' up to 5ft (1.5m) in length, these very large shawls were often folded in half, then folded over again at the top for extra warmth. Not only were Norwich shawls famous for their quality, but many were made in a very distinctive and striking colour of Norwich Red or Turkey Red, a dye originally developed by the Norwich chemist William Stark. The highest quality shawls in the city were produced by Towler & Campin and were of a woven silk gauze called leno. They had a band of thick ribbed weaving just in from the edge which helped to prevent the delicate shawl from tearing. During the heyday of the Norwich shawl

Townsend's Monthly Selection of Parisian costumes, June 1844.

in the 1840s, a working couple could earn as much as £15 a week as outworkers and there were at least twenty-eight manufacturers producing shawls in the city at this time. One firm, E. & F. Hinde, made no less than twenty-six different types of shawl and were producing some 39,000 shawls every year.

There were numerous other forms of outerwear, with multitudinous names. There was the Camail, a waist-length cloak with arm holes, a rounded neck and small falling collar, often made from muslin, cashmere or velvet and usually fringed; the Crispin, was a short mantle, occasionally with sleeves, worn close around the shoulders with a small pelerine cape; the Crispin Cloche was a knee-length, bell-shaped Crispin; the Cardinal, a short collarless cape without sleeves hanging just above or just below waist level, often made of lace for evening wear; the Polverino, a large, loose and unlined cloak with or without a hood and often of silk; the Casaweck, a short mantle, lined, wadded and quilted at the border; the Polish jacket, generally of cashmere and lined with quilted satin, it was waist-length with revers and a collar similar to a man's dress coat and sleeves slit to the elbow, it was usually worn at the seaside or in the country. There were paletot and pardessus too, many of these names were often interchangeable and by the late 1840s the generic term 'mantle' was often used.

The well-dressed lady was never seen without a hat to compliment her outfit. When Queen Victoria was crowned in 1837 the fashion was for a bonnet with a wide brim attached to a large deep crown tilting up from the back of the head, this was tied under the chin with a wide ribbon, pulling the brim around to frame the face. There was a 'bavolet', a curtain of fabric, attached to the base of the crown which covered the neck. These large brimmed bonnets gave way to what became known as the poke bonnet. The brim narrowed and lowered down to below chin level, the crown also lowered creating a funnel shape which totally concealed the face from the side and impaired the wearer's vision. The inner edging of the bonnet was lined and decorated, framing the face with artificial flowers, feathers, ribbons and lace, 'no one article in the whole range of female costume is more important in its effects than the comparatively small piece of satin, silk or other material that forms the lining of the bonnet.'[17]

The flowers that were used to decorate the bonnets were usually real ones, so not only were they decorative but they would have an added fragrance, in March 1841 *The World of Fashion* reported: 'We have seen several bonnets decorated with curled ostrich feathers, twisted at the ends; the interior of the brims are decorated with small tufts of marguerites, honeysuckle, lilacs and violets.' There were also bonnets of 'pale pink pou de soie, ornamented, or rather we should say, partially covered with English pointlace, tastefully arranged, and attached on one side by a bouquet of hyacinths, of a deeper shade of red than the bonnet.'[18]

The bonnets themselves were made from materials like horsehair, rush, straw, wool, silk and velvet. From the beginning of the seventeenth century, England had a thriving straw hat industry based in the counties of Bedfordshire, Hertfordshire and Buckinghamshire. The straw grown in that region had a fine bright colour and local women and children were employed in their own homes to create straw plaits that could be turned into fashionable bonnets, attending specialist schools to learn the trade. However, the best quality and most sought after and expensive Leghorn straw came from Tuscany, Italy.

One aptly named innovation of the late 1840s was the 'ugly'. This was an extension worn round the brim of the bonnet to protect the wearer from the sun and was basically fabric stretched over cane supports forming a detachable brim worn with the bonnet. The name is said to have come from a comment made in *Punch* in 1848. The decade saw the beginning of a slow move away from the bonnet. A low-crowned, circular-brimmed hat could sometimes be seen, particularly at the seaside or in the country, its function being to shade the wearer's face and neck.

A woman's crowning glory is said to be her hair and in the early 1840s hairstyles were neat, centre parted with side ringlets over the ears; very reminiscent of Carolean women's hairstyles of the seventeenth century, that filled much of the funnel of the bonnet. Over subsequent years the centre parting remained but the hair at the side was drawn down over the front of the ear then looped up into a bun at the back of the head. Haircare was also important and, just like today, there were many tips to keep it looking beautiful. For drying long hair *Handbook of the Toilette* recommended the use of the vapours of 'gum benjamin' (a corrupted name for benzoin), a fragrant tree resin with a sweet vanilla like smell. The lady is instructed to,

> recline in a chaise longue or sofa, with her long hair hanging over the end. A pan containing two or three bits of ignited charcoal is then placed under it, and a little powdered benzoin sprinkled upon the lighted fuel. The thick smoke which rises and is strongly impregnated with benzoic acid, combined with carbonic acid, rapidly absorbs the moisture in the hair, which should be previously well wiped with towels, so as to be as free from wet as possible; and in a few seconds the hair is perfectly dry, beautifully perfumed, and ready for the operation of the brush.[19]

The *Handbook* goes on to give advice on dying the hair using a powder made from litharge (a natural mineral form of lead(II) oxide) and quicklime (Calcium Oxide). This is mixed with hot water to form a cream which is then thickly applied to the head from the roots to the tips. The hair should then 'be covered with porous brown paper saturated with hot water and secured by an ample oil skin cap', and left on the head for three to eight hours depending on the colour required. Apparently this mixture would produce a 'yellow auburn and four distinct shades from light brown to black.'[20] After the desired amount of time the cap was removed and the loose powder shaken out, the remainder being left in the hair till dry and then brushed out. Almost as an aside, the book mentions that it is advisable not to inhale the dust as it may irritate the lungs. We now understand that quicklime reacts with water and can cause severe irritation to skin, lungs and eyes, this chemical reaction can also release enough heat to ignite combustible materials!

Eyelashes that were considered too pale could also be dyed to give more definition to the eye. To do this you needed the help of someone with a steady hand. With the eyes closed, a piece of flat wood is placed under the lashes and each is coloured with a fine black lead pencil. This, however, was a temporary solution, for a more permanent colour, 'each eyelash should be touched with a strong aqueous solution of carbonate of soda applied with a fine camel hair pencil. As soon as lashes are dry a little marking ink for linen should be applied carefully.'[21]

With ears being covered by the hair, the large earrings that had been popular fell out of fashion as they could no longer be seen. The shape of the bonnet also evolved, becoming rounder and worn well back, once again revealing the face. The bavolet was retained, but trimmings moved around the bonnet to the sides, ribbon rosettes and curling ostrich plumes became popular as well as seasonal flowers.

In early Victorian times respectable married women covered their heads not only outdoors, but indoors too, with a morning or indoor cap. This had been a fashion for decades and there appears to be no reason for this other than a lady did not feel properly dressed unless she had something on her head, and outdoor bonnets were not appropriate for indoor use. Generally made of fine lawn or muslin and trimmed with embroidery, frills, net or lace insertions. Caps of the 1840s were close fitting with frills and ribbons hanging down over the ears in the from of lappets. They would be worn on their own indoors, and under the bonnet outdoors. Women would also wear wrist-length, soft buff, or kid gloves indoors, ostensibly to preserve the texture and colour of the hands, which would only be removed when at table.

As the skirts dropped to ground-length again, women's feet once again

Note the long tight bodice with revers de pelerine (pleats) running from shoulder to waistline, helping create the illusion of a narrow waist, and the unusual indoor cap c.1844.

disappeared from view. For indoors there was the popular square-toed satin slipper, often with a small buckle or rosette on the toe and usually in black or white, dress boots in coloured silks were also popular. For venturing outdoors, half-boots were worn; these were flat heeled, side laced and made in a number of materials including fabric and leather. In 1837, J. Sparkes Hall, Queen Victoria's bootmaker, had patented an elastic-sided boot, presenting it to the queen the same year. By 1843 'J. Sparkes-Hall's Patent Elastic Ankle Boot' was being advertised in the *Illustrated London News* with claims that the boots,

> require neither lacing, buttoning, nor tying; they can be put on and off in a moment without trouble or loss of time. The constant annoyance of laces breaking, buttons coming off, holes wearing out, and many other imperfections in the ordinary modes of fastening, suggested the improvement which is now submitted to the public.[22]

Much worn by Victoria, they are still around today; we know them under their far simpler nom-de-plume of Chelsea Boots.

In colder weather ladies could wear silk, cashmere or woollen gaiters, or the the newly invented and even more practical India rubber gaiter that was advertised in 1840. For particularly wet weather rubber galoshes (overshoes) were also a relatively new invention. In November 1840, Mr J. Fiddaman, a Wholesale Carrier of Bridge Street, Newark, was advertising a large stock of 'India Rubber Goloshes', according to the advert he had,

> a large stock of the improved India rubber shoes adapted for the present season; and he takes this opportunity to inform the nobility and gentry of the Midland Counties of the fact, that they are now become so general that J.F. Deems any comment quite unnecessary.' Any lady or gentleman may receive than at any distance by enclosing an old boot or shoe, with a remittance for the same.[23]

Jewellery

During the Romantic Period of the 1830s and 1840s there were several factors that influenced taste in jewellery. Not only was there an interest in all things gothic and medieval, but people were also fascinated by ancient archaeology; the influence of the ancient civilisations of Greece, Rome and Egypt can be seen in jewellery designs of the time in the form of lotus flowers, tassels and knot-work. Coral became very popular, remaining so till the mid-1860s. It could be worn in its natural form, a custom brought over from Italy that was believed to ward off the evil eye, or, as was often the case, finely carved into motifs such as flowers, beads and crosses. The colours of coral varied, the most popular were dark red and pale pink, in 1840 *World of Fashion* reported how coral was used to decorate ball gowns: 'elegant trimming is composed of coral sprigs arranged in the form of a wreath on each side of the front of a ball dress, and terminated by floating sprigs.'[24]

Jewellery of the last years of the 1830s and into the 1840s often drew on the natural world for inspiration. You can find jewellery in the form of leaves, birds and seed pearls arranged as clusters of berries. On the announcement of their engagement in 1839, Prince Albert presented Queen Victoria with an engagement ring. This was unusual in Britain, engagement rings were seldom given as a betrothal of love to fiancées at the time, and the ring he gave her would be considered unconventional even by today's standards. Made in of 18 carat gold, it was shaped like a serpent with rubies for eyes, diamonds for the mouth and a large emerald set in the centre, the latter being Victoria's birth stone. The ring was designed by Albert and it is believed that Victoria was wearing it when she was buried. Today it may seem an unusual choice for an engagement ring, but the snake in Victorian times represented love, wisdom and eternity, and was a particularly popular token of affection.

The young Victoria influenced the nation's taste in jewellery in other ways too. She had particular love for cameos and consequently these enjoyed a huge resurgence in popularity. Her love of Scotland also had an impact when the royal couple purchased Balmoral in 1848, and Victoria started collecting and wearing the multi-coloured Scottish Cairngorm agate jewellery, both in silver and cheaper plated mounts, it became the must-have souvenir for anyone visiting Scotland. Bracelets were also popular throughout the decade, from multiple bracelets worn on both arms, to broad ones on their own. Small brooches were common and in the early 1840s there was a vogue for wearing a small bottle, containing either perfume or smelling salts, suspended by a chain and hook from the waist.

The industrialisation during the reign of Queen Victoria also extended to the manufacture of jewellery. Where previously it had all been meticulously made by hand, mechanisation saw an increase in cheaper more affordable items. A cheaper alternative to gold commonly known as pinchbeck had been available since the early eighteenth century, but it became very popular in the early years of Victoria's reign. It was an alloy of copper and zinc that simulated gold and was used extensively with paste or inexpensive stones until the early 1850s. Its demise was brought about by two things: first, the development of electro-gilded base metals in the 1840s, which revolutionised the production of costume jewellery making it both cheaper and quicker to produce. Second, in 1854, the carat standard of gold in England was lowered. The carat represents the percentage of gold in an item, the higher the carat, the higher the gold content and consequently its price. For over 200 years 22ct and 18ct were the two standards available, 1854 saw the introduction of 15ct, 12ct and 9ct, the latter being 37 per cent pure gold, thus making gold jewellery affordable for many more people.

Fabrics and colours of the 1840s

Some of the most common fabrics and popular colours as recorded in fashion magazines, pattern books and adverts of the 1840s:

Algerine, alpaca, alpago, balzarine, barathea, barège beche-cachemire, broché moiré cambric, cashmere, cashmere syrien, chiné plaids, coburgs, cordelière, crêpe, damasks, foulards (plain, satin striped, plaid), gauze, gingham (striped), grenadine, gros de Naples, gros de Orient, jacconet, levatine, merino (plain, quadrilled in satin), mousseline de laine, muslin, nankin, oiseau satin royal, oiseau velvet, organdy (plain, embroidered, printed with small patterns), Orleans cloth, ottoman silk, paramatta, pekin chiné, pekin Victoria, percaline, plaid, pompadour chiné, poplin, poplin broché, poult de soie, radzimir, rep, rep-bluets, satin (broché, merino, moiré, with velvet stripes), satin pompadour, satin Turc, Saxony cloth, silk (quadrilled, plaided, marbled, watered, chiné, checked, figured, glacé, shot), sarsenet, taffeta (shot, quadrilled, striped, plaid), tarlatan, terry velvet, tulle, velour frisé, velvet.

Apricot, azure blue, black, blue, bottle green, brown, cherry, crimson, dark blue, dark green, drab, emerald green, fawn, garnet, gold, green, grey, Indian green, lavender, light green, light violet, lilac, marron, marsh mallow, orange, pale blue, pale pink, pale primrose, pale orange, pea green, peach shot with black, pensée, pink, porcelain blue, puce, rose, rose de chine, sea green, slate, straw, Victoria Blue, violet, white, yellow.

Stripes were popular, patterns were generally larger than in the previous decade.

Horizontal bodice decoration was very fashionable, as were the wide pagoda sleeves, although these were usually worn with separate white under sleeves, 'engageantes', c.1854.

Chapter 2

1850s

The 1850s began with The Great Exhibition of the Works of Industry of All Nations (more succinctly known as The Great Exhibition) at Crystal Palace, London. More than half the 100,000 exhibits showcased British (and British Empire) manufacturing at its best, including fabrics, clothing, ironwork, pottery, furniture, perfumes, pianos, firearms, steam hammers and hydraulic presses. The exhibition ran from May to October 1851 and had over 6 million visitors. Britain was one of the most industrially advanced countries in the world, by the early 1850s there were thousands of steam-powered looms churning out millions of miles of fabric every year.

In the days before synthetic fibres the looms produced wool, silk, linen and cotton fabrics as well as mixes such as silk and wool, wool and cotton. There were different weights of fabrics for each season and prices to suit most pockets. Much of the richer more expensive fabrics were purchased from France, and the gradual industrialisation there saw the cost of these drop considerably.

The Guidebook for the Industrial Exhibition of 1851 records that in Britain at the time there were 1,497 factories producing woollen cloth housing 9,499 powered looms and employing 74,448 people; worsted factories numbered 501 with 32,617 powered looms and 79,737 employees; silk factories numbered 277 with 6,092 powered looms and 42,544 employees; cotton factories numbered 1,932, with 249,627 powered looms and 330,924 employees; linen factories numbered 393 with 1,141 powered looms and 33,434 employees. Britain's output was vast, although not all was for the domestic market, and choice was huge. At the Great Exhibition a single exhibitor, Messrs. H.J. & D. Nicoll of Regent Street, merchant clothiers and manufacturers of cloth, exhibited upwards of 200 varieties of woollen cloth in numerous colours, textures and finishes.

Fashion Magazines

The rapid industrialisation of the nineteenth century also saw advances in the processes involved in both paper manufacture and printing, the growth of railroads lead to improved distribution and the postal service expanded. These advances, as well as increasing literacy among women, combined to create a burgeoning market for women's magazines. In 1850 there were nine fashion magazines being published from London, including *World of Fashion Monthly Magazine of the Courts of London and Paris* (in 1850 the first to include paper patterns), *La Belle Assemblée*, *The Lady's Gazette of Fashion* and *The Ladies' Cabinet of Fashion, Music and Romance,* by the end of the decade a further five were in circulation. Many of the earlier ones were aimed at the wealthier end of society.

In 1852 Samuel Beeton created *The Englishwoman's Domestic Magazine* the first cheap magazine for young middle-class women and it was an immediate success. Rather than simply a fashion magazine its contents covered a wide variety of useful topics including gardening, medical advice, recipes and cooking tips, serialised stories and embroidery. There were hints and tips on dressmaking and advice on what to wear; the magazine contained not only high quality fashion plates purchased from *Le Moniteur des Modes* (a weekly French fashion magazine), but also paper dressmaking patterns. Most young middle-class girls were taught to sew, embroider, crochet and tat and were given an understanding of fabrics and how they 'work' by older female relatives, or if they were lucky enough, their tutors. The availability of up-to-the minute fashion patterns negated the expense of using a professional dressmaker and allowed more women to create their own wardrobe.

The 1850s Look

Dresses initially retained the line of the 1840s and overall the hallmark look of the 1850s was one of neatness and modesty. Some say this reflected the ideal of womanhood propounded at the time. Subtle changes were taking place though. The decade saw the introduction of the front fastening, or jacket, bodice which gradually gained in popularity. The back-fastening bodice and skirt had become two separate items giving the appearance of a dress. This meant the skirt could be worn for different occasions as different bodices could be made to be worn with it. For daytime the bodice could have a high neckline worn with a small detachable white collar of lace, tatting or crochet, or a 'V' neckline which would be filled with a white 'chemisette'. For an evening ball the neckline could be low, and it could be worn off the shoulder, with short sleeves. The fabric in the bodice was gathered or pleated from the shoulders to the waistline forming a V-shape, this gave the impression that the shoulders were wider and the waist narrower than they were. This V shape was wider than that of the previous decade. Similarly, 'bretelles' were a broader, cape-like arrangement which extended beyond the shoulders, but again tapered down to a V at the waist, these were common from around 1856–58 and were often trimmed with fringing.

Bodices were, in general, more embellished than before and in the the early 1850s there was a fashion for horizontal decoration across the front. Towards the end of the decade fringing became a popular trim, the *Illustrated London News* commented that the 'fringe may be said to be the most becoming of all trimmings for a lady's dress; it seems to possess the power of importing lightness and suppleness to the movements of the wearer.[1]

Within the fringing you could also find small silk-covered balls, tassels, pearls or beads to enhance decoration, and fringing could be applied to skirts in horizontal rows to simulate flounces.

The 'basque' becomes popular in the early years of the decade, this is an extension sewn onto the bodice which flares over the hips. The 'basquin' was the same but was cut as an integral part of the bodice. Popular throughout the rest of the decade they can be seen in various forms, the edges could be plain, decorated or fringed. Plain bodices

Detachable white collars were popular on high necked day dresses. 'Bretelles' were a cape-like arrangement extending beyond the shoulders and tapering to a V at the waist, c.1856.

with straight waists and without 'basques' were also to be seen, and around 1857 they were often worn with a belt and buckle, or a broad ribbon with floating ends, the latter usually on lighter summer dresses. The waistline, after having been quite low in the 1840s, gradually crept upwards, being at the natural waist or just below in the early 1850s and settling at a straight, natural waistline by 1860.

The 1850s saw a variety of sleeve shapes, one of the most common being the pagoda sleeve. This was narrow at the top, though not tight, widening to a funnel shape at the wrist, becoming very wide from around 1857. The pagoda sleeve could have a closed seam to the wrist or, quite often, was split up the front either to the elbow or nearly all the way to the shoulder and trimmed with ruching or fringing. The pagoda could also be made of two or three wide bias-cut flounces and by the end of the decade the fullness could fall directly from the armhole. No matter its construction, it was always worn with white cambric, linen, muslin, lace or net 'engageantes' underneath, sometimes they were quite voluminous and filled the sleeve, and always ended in a neat cuff. The 'engageantes' were required under all wide sleeves to cover the bare arm during the daytime and were separate from the bodice, either tying or buttoning to the inside of the sleeve, making them easily removable for cleaning. By mid-decade, sleeves had started to become more closed at the wrists.

A bishop sleeve consisting of a closed, full sleeve, gathered into a narrow cuff became popular in the mid-1850s. There were also seldom seen styles including the Amadis sleeve, which was set into the armholes in large pleats concealed by an epaulette, it was close fitting, ending in a deep cuff and was often worn with a plain bodice; the Gabrielle sleeve, where the fabric was gathered into two or three puffs from the shoulder to the wrist ending in a cuff; the Grecian sleeve was slit open along one side but closed with buttons and worn as an under sleeve as a change from the full 'egageantes'. By the end of the decade all sleeves had a sleeve cap, or epaulette, at the top which accentuated the drooping shoulders and was often decorated with braid, cording or beads. For evening wear the trend throughout the 1850s was for short fitting sleeves with a lace edging, or slightly longer elbow-length ones with lace ruffles.

The most distinctive feature of late 1840s and early 1850s fashions were the ever-widening skirt. The width the skirt could attain was limited by the bulk of the petticoats at the waist. Both design and fabric were used to give the impression of width and rows of flounces, wide frills round the skirt started appearing to further increase the perceived circumference. The fashion journals proclaimed that 'flounces are very generally worn; on all thin materials they are indispensable'.[2] The number of flounces seen would often depend on the fabric and could be made of the same fabric as the dress or of a contrasting one. Sometimes there was just a single, knee-length flounce, but multiples were more common. On lighter fabrics, flounces were narrower and more numerous, you could find six, seven or more, their edges could be straight or scalloped and were often pinked. Pinking, cutting a series of tiny 'v' shapes along the edges, was a way of reducing fraying in un-hemmed fabrics.

If the flounces were numerous they could often overlap slightly so the actual fabric of the skirt was not seen, it was therefore possible to use a different, less expensive material to make this. Medium materials would carry two or three broad flounces, and heavy fabrics no more than two; they could be edged in velvet, chenille fringing or with ruching. The edges of any weight fabric could have a horizontal band of colour or design

The closed bishop sleeve was becoming popular as was the sleeve cap, the width of the skirt is emphasised by one large flounce, c.1856.

The addition of ruffles and horizontal bands of contrasting fabric were used to emphasise the width of the skirt, c.1854.

woven into them, and appliquéd Greek style 'key' patterns were popular. Decoration was added 'à disposition', that is in horizontal border patterns for the flounces to further emphasise width. Around about mid-decade flounces stuck out a little as they were given a stiff muslin backing. A further flounce was formed by the 'basque' of the jacket bodice over the hips and was often decorated with the same horizontal design as that on the skirt. The top flounce would often conceal a pocket. By the early 1860s, flounces were mostly a fashion of the past.

The introduction of the crinoline cage mid-decade not only changed the shape of the skirt but also altered the construction. The skirts of the 1840s and 1850s were made from large oblongs of fabric which, when sewn together, did not sit so well over the crinoline cage and created bulk at the waist. These problems were both eliminated by the introduction of gores, whereby the skirt was constructed with inserted triangular panels rather than just straight widths of fabric, thus creating width at the bottom but narrowness at the waist. Gathers or large pleats could still be used at the back, but the skirt would now sit much more smoothly over the cage. The crinoline negated the need for the additional flounces, but it seems they hung on till at least 1858 as *Ladies Treasury* points out:

> although the plain skirt is adopted, many skirts are still to be seen profusely trimmed, but seldom or never down the side. The trimmings are placed round the skirt, and they are of the same colour as the dress. Even one flounce has found favour in some eyes, and rich trimmings down the front of the skirt are in vogue.[3]

Foundation Garments

By the 1850s petticoats would frequently have a band of whalebone or horsehair at the hem, or had rows of very thin whalebone up to the knees to try and hold them in shape. For the skirt to retain the required shape, multiple layers of cotton petticoats were required; these were heavy, cumbersome, impeded movement and were hot in the summer. For warmth in winter, quilted petticoats lined with wadding added a further encumbrance. To try to alleviate this, dressmakers also started to insert whalebone into the dresses themselves.

Note the high waist emphasised, with a ribbon, and the pinked edges of the skirt ruffles, 1850.

Use of the crinoline cage meant ruffles around the skirt were no longer required to give it width, c1857.

The real step forward happened in 1855 with the introduction of a garment that would remove the need for layers of petticoats and allow skirts to reach their widest circumference. The item of clothing in question was the crinoline cage. These were constructed with cane, whalebone or wire hoops, increasing in size as they got closer to the feet. These hoops were either encased in a linen or cotton petticoat, or held in place horizontally by vertical tapes, thus creating the 'cage' look. A petticoat was worn underneath, but a single cotton petticoat with a flounced hem was all that was needed over the top, although two would generally ensure it's outline would be hidden. The bell-shaped skirt formed by multiple layers of petticoats was now a thing of the past, the skirt had become a dome.

A popular story tells of how the crinoline was first brought to England by Empress Eugénie, wife of Napoleon III, when they visited Queen Victoria at Windsor in April 1855. Sadly, there is no solid proof of this, though women had been looking for a more comfortable way to support their ever-growing skirts, so it is probable the fashion would have arrived here sooner rather than later, particularly because it would have been picked up by the fashion magazines of the time. There is no doubt though, that Eugénie's wearing of the cage encouraged its use, there are even adverts in the papers at the time for the 'Parisian Eugénie Jupon Skeleton Petticoat'. No matter who introduced it to Britain, the crinoline cage was destined to shape skirts for much of the decade.

In 1857, a new process enabled the use of sprung steel, which keeps its form despite bending, to give the cage its shape, and it was still very much lighter than the layers of petticoat previously worn. The cage was comfortable, kept the petticoats away from the legs, making walking easier, and swung in an elegant manner, often flashing the ankles so a fashion for coloured stockings also emerged. The crinoline cage was cheap and quick to produce and was soon adopted by all classes. In photographs of the time you can occasionally make out the outline of the cage beneath the skirt, and the ever-growing crinoline cage became a target for satirical cartoonists in *Punch* who dubbed the craze 'Crinolinemania'.

The decade also saw improvements to the corset, making it more wearer-friendly. For obvious reasons, the back-fastening corset was not ideal and in 1829 Frenchman Jean Julien Josselin patented a two-part steel busk. However, this proved rather unpopular because it did not always fasten securely and had a tendency to spring open. It was not until 1848, when Joseph Cooper patented the 'slot and stud' fastening busk, still in use today, that the problem was resolved and the popularity of the front-fastening corset really took off in the 1850s.

The adoption of the front-fastening busk led to the spiral lacing of the back fastening corset being replaced with lacing *à la paresseuse*, also called 'lazy lacing', which allowed the wearer to tighten her own corset. Rather than the one lace spiralling down from top to bottom, the corset was now laced in a manner that produced two large loops at either side of the waist. These could be pulled tighter by the wearer, tied around the waist and finally tucked under a hook on the lower front of the corset to prevent an unsightly bulge at the waist.

These developments meant women could put on and take off their own corsets without assistance, they were eminently practical for every woman, especially those who did not have the luxury of servants and were widely adopted as the standard fastening for women's corsets from the late 1850s.

The tighter lacing of the 1840s continued until the adoption of the crinoline. This is partly because the loss of the huge gigot sleeves of the 1830s removed the optical illusion of the tiny waist, which was deemed highly desirable. The tighter lacing of the corset was a way of compensating for this. The crinoline, however, once again made the waist look smaller, and tighter lacing fell out of fashion.

Exactly how small was the 'tight-laced' waist of the 1840s–1850s, and later the 1880s when tight lacing was once again fashionable? Women were smaller and slimmer, some would prefer their corsets tighter laced than others, some may even reduce their measurements through vanity, but did they all have that much-quoted 18-inch waist? In 1949 Doris Langley Moore, founder of The Fashion Museum in Bath, measured hundreds of dresses and bodices of the Victorian period from collections across the country. Measuring these rather than the corsets themselves would give a better idea of average waist sizes simply because a corset was not laced till the edges met, there was a varying gap of inches at the back. Her findings indicate that hardly any women had a waist of less than 21 inches with many falling in the 20- to 30-inch range. This is upheld by the Victoria and Albert Museum who similarly measured their corsets laced closed. Average measurements were between 21 and 26½ inches, bearing in mind that the average gap at the back was 2–4 inches, this gives an average waist measurement of between 23–30 inches. Really tight lacing was a choice, one that most women would not make.

Reading through the newspapers of the decade there are numerous adverts for corsetry, many of which use the believed health benefits of new designs and materials as a selling point. There is the Royal Adelaide Corset, the Patent Eumorphon Corset, which is 'approved by the whole of the medical profession',[4] as well as Madam Elan and her Hygienic & French corsets, Juvenile corsets, walking and riding corsets, back and front, double Mechanic Self Adjusting, and chest-relieving corsets. Then there is the McLintock & Co Improved Elastic Corsets:

> no lady who has any regard for symmetry and constitutional health should be without them…. They never unnaturally confine they physical constitution; but on the contrary, are fully adapted, from their elasticity, to permit the most perfect freedom of respiration and motion. NB An inspection of the newly invented Universal Fit and

Chest Expanding Elastic Corset is solicited. The most eminent of the faculty recommend them in preference to any yet invented. Warranted not to lose their elastic; also to allow of washing with hot water and soap, and well brushing without sustaining the least injury.'[5]

Similarly the Corset de la Cour Francaise advertised in 1850 had the 'finest elastic threads introduced into the material', these responded to the 'slightest and most delicate respiratory action of the lungs ... and the circulation is rather promoted than impeded'.'

In the advert the claims of the latter are supported by statements from various medical and ladies journals from the *Lancet* to *Lady's Newspaper*.

By this time the corset no longer had shoulder straps and, with the use of gores, flared out to end several inches below the waist giving a more curvaceous figure. Continuing improvements in mechanisation meant that by the mid-1850s the ready-made, mass-produced corset was widely available. The display dedicated to the corset at the Great Exhibition in 1851 awarded prizes for the most innovative. A report after the exhibition reads:

> In the general trade, within the last four or five years, the make and shape of these articles have been greatly improved, so that there can now be obtained by all classes, a well-formed and good corset at a very moderate price; a large quantity are now woven by machinery.[6]

The long voluminous, simple chemise from the previous decade with its short sleeves and square neckline was still worn under the corset but the 1850s saw the adoption of corset covers. These had started appearing in the 1840s but only became widely worn throughout this decade. These were shaped bodices worn over the corset but under the dress and they helped to soften the edges of the corset so that they did not show through the bodice. For everyday wear they were made of linen or batiste, from silk or satin for the evening and from merino or flannel for winter and by the end of the century were known as camisoles.

Despite their introduction early in the nineteenth century, prior to the appearance of the crinoline cage drawers, or pantalettes, were not always worn. However, the adoption of the cage necessitated them for warmth and modesty, should the cage unexpectedly swing too high, and the wearing of drawers became the norm. They were long, voluminous, and worn well below the knee, and like those that were worn in previous decades, open along the crotch seams. Initially relatively plain, all white underwear gradually become more decorative, often with embroidery, lace and tucks. For colder weather there were regular adverts in the newspapers for merino and lambs' wool vests and drawers, the former worn over the corset. The new technology of machine knitting, as demonstrated at The Great Exhibition in 1851, created a finer gauge of knitting, allowing knitted garments to fit more snugly to the figure.

Queen Victoria and Balmoral

In the autumn of 1842 Queen Victoria paid her first visit to Scotland. So enamoured were she and Prince Albert with the Highlands that six years later they took out a lease on Balmoral and purchased it in 1852. In the 1850s the name 'Balmoral' was given to various items of warm, sensible clothing associated with the Royal Family when they stayed in Scotland. The Balmoral petticoat was one of them. It was made from red wool and had two to four black stripes running around the hem. It was designed to show below the skirts which were looped up about a foot at every seam when out walking or taking part in sports, such as croquet, which were starting to increase in popularity among women later in this decade. In *Habits of Good Society* (1855) it was noted that 'Victoria has assumed the Balmoral petticoat, than which, for health, comfort, warmth and effect, no invention was ever better. She has courageously accompanied with the Balmoral boot, and even with the mohair and coloured stockings.'[7]

The somewhat inclement weather of Scotland induced the young queen to look for something more substantial in the way of footwear. Her simple answer was to adopt the Balmoral boot which had been designed for Prince Albert as a walking boot. It was waterproof, tough enough to wear out and about on the estate, but also smart enough to wear indoors. Consequently, with the royal couple wearing them, the Balmoral boot became extremely popular with the gentry. In February 1859 *Punch* had this to say about the influence of Balmoral on clothing:

As for thin shoes, except for dancing they appear to have vanished from the female toilet. 'Balmoral' boots, soled half an inch thick, and military heels, have usurped their place. These boots and the martial red petticoats now so familiar to the eye, are to me eloquent manifestations of the change that has come over the spirit of womanhood.

The scandalous Miss Bloomer – Amelia Jenks Bloomer

Mrs Amelia Bloomer lived in Seneca Falls in New York State. Her husband, whom she had married in 1840, was both a local judge and postmaster. Soon after her marriage she started to produce *The Lily*, a paper mainly concerned with temperance and literature, but becoming famous for its support of women's rights, and particularly the new costume its author recommended. The costume in question, Turkish pantaloons and knee-length skirt, was originally worn by Mrs Elizabeth Smith Miller, but it was not until Mrs Bloomer took it up and slightly modified the idea, promoting it in *The Lily*, that it caught public attention. The *Northern Standard* of 23 August 1851 reports that in America, Independence Day had seen a number of American cities graced by the presence of ladies in the 'Bloomer costume'. In Akron, Ohio, over sixty ladies sported the outfit, and in Lowell, Massachusetts, all the factory girls turned out for the procession clad à la Bloomer.

Amelia Bloomer wearing her daring 'Bloomer costume', c1850.

The *Illustrated London News* described the outfit:

Leaving the portion above the waist to the taste of the wearer, suggesting however, that it should be much looser and less constraining to the motions of the arms and chest than it now is, we would have a skirt reaching down to nearly half way between the knee and ankle, and not made quite so full as is the present fashion. Underneath the skirt, trousers moderately full, in fair, mild weather, coming down to the ankle – not instep – and there gathered with an elastic band. The shoes or slippers to suit the occasion. For winter, or wet weather, the trousers also full, but coming down into a boot, which should rise some three or four inches at least above the ankle.[8]

The article took pains to point out the trousers of the outfit were an 'essential part of the habitual dress; the skirt an addition for grace and propriety'. The paper goes on to explain that the new outfit would be cheaper as it uses less fabric than the current fashions, would be conducive to good health by 'the avoidance of damp skirts hanging about the feet and ankles, since they would be clad in a boot',[9] and the fabrics used could be better adapted to the seasons, making it cooler in the summer and warmer in the winter.

The outfit was so unusual there was quite a flurry of interest and curiosity around it. In October 1851 the London Bloomer Committee was formed, a lecture was to be given later that month at the Royal Soho Theatre at which it claimed:

resolutions will be proposed, which the mothers and daughters of England are earnestly invited to attend, and by their presence forward the welfare of the present and future generations, by adopting an improved method instead of the present injurious and artificial mode of dress'[10]

The new outfit was deemed to be more comfortable, healthier and to provide unimpeded movement; the ladies of the Committee attended in full Bloomer costume. Lectures were also given in other London theatres, in Dublin and Glasgow, although with regards to the latter, the *Illustrated London News* states that 'although the men appear in petticoats north of the Tweed, that is no reason why the fair sex should adopt 'continuations'.[11] The new outfit was supported by the *Medical Times* who said:

it becomes a mere question of common sense whether a costume which clothes the body well and yet allows free play to every part, is not a more rational habit than a pinched-up, wasp like waist, and a cumbersome mass of horse-hair, hoops, furbelows, and flounces, sweeping the mud in the streets.[12]

However, the outfit also received criticism for being unfeminine, to which the *Illustrated London News* had this to say:

In reply to the objection of unsexing, it is maintained that the dress need have no masculine characteristics about it. The costume of the Polish ladies and the out-door-dress of the Russians – which, resembling each other very much, I should take as the proper types for our ladies to model theirs upon – has surely never been obnoxious to such a charge; while the Turkish women have always been considered, in physique and in costume, as the embodiment of all that is feminine.[13]

Another story recounted how an elderly lady believed she was too old to adopt the new costume, Amelia Bloomer told her:

Do just as your impulses move you to do. What you find a burden in belief or apparel, cast off. Woman has always sacrificed her comfort for fashion. You old women of sixty have been slaves to the tyrant long enough, and as you have but a few years to live, be as free and as happy as you can in what time remains.[14]

So why did the Bloomer costume not catch on? Despite a certain amount of support, the outfit was so different to what had gone before that it became a prime target for ridicule, many wits and notable magazines such as *Punch* took great pleasure in lampooning both the outfit and Amelia herself. Street hawkers sold cartoons with badly written verse attached to them, Madame Tussaud even added a group of figures in Bloomer costume to her exhibition. Had the young queen adopted the new look, there is no doubt that its popularity would have spread; as it was, no self-respecting lady would be seen dressed in such an outfit, it was 'killed by ridicule and satire'. Mrs Merrifield in her book *Dress as a Fine Art*, also suggested that a reason for its failure was that 'we are content to adopt the greatest absurdities in dress when they are brought from Paris, or recommended by a French name; but American fashions have no chance of success in aristocratic England.'[15] However, with hindsight we can say that Mrs Bloomer was forty years ahead of her time, for in the 1890s the Bloomer would make a reappearance.

Accessories

Due to the ever-expanding skirts shawls were still very popular. At the Great Exhibition in 1851, Norwich manufacturers displayed their beautiful shawls, much impressing Queen Victoria who ordered two, further cementing Norwich's reputation for quality. In 1854 Norwich-based Clabburn, Sons & Crisp solved a long-standing 'problem' with the shawl – the right and wrong side – by producing the first reversible shawl. The shawl's popularity would carry on throughout the 1850s and 1860s, fading as the huge skirts deflated and by 1870 its heyday was over.

As with the previous decade, there were numerous variations on a theme for outer garments that were fitted to the waist falling under the general

Fashions of London & Paris, January 1857.

term 'pardessus', which remained fashionable. Cloaks for walking were popular, they were generally rounded and either plain or trimmed with braid or plush, with a tasselled hood. There was even a short Balmoral cloak with a narrow hood, and a burnoose-type cloak for evenings, with a hood and a profusion of tassels. Mantles were fitted across the shoulder often hanging to the knee with a fringed or lace edging and armholes cut lengthways and edged. The Pelisse could be short with large pleats at the back and sides to accommodate the skirt, or knee-length and gored at the waist to fit over the skirt, often trimmed with fur or velvet. The 'casaque' was close fitting, buttoning to the neck, with 'basques' lying flat over the skirt. The pelisse mantle was double breasted, buttoning down the front with a flat collar and short wide sleeves, it was knee-length and often had pockets. The caracao was a loose-fitting jacket worn open to the waist over a chemisette, some with wide reveres and very often made from a different fabric to the skirt. The second-half of the decade saw a loose-fitting jacket become very popular. It was relatively plain, fell more or less straight from the shoulder, had wide sleeves and could be short or three quarter length.

Headwear was still very much a requirement throughout the decade. The tunnel-like poke bonnets of the 1840s gradually saw both their crown and brim shorten and the whole thing moved towards the back of the head, once again revealing the face and hair, with the 'bavolet' remaining firmly in place throughout and only varying in length. The 'spoon' bonnet was characterised by a straight line from crown to brim then a sharp upward slant with sides that curved down at jaw level.

Bonnets were made from felt, velvet and straw, the interior of the brim was often decorated, framing the face. Early on, the tulle and flower decorations were beside the cheeks, but as the bonnet opened up they became more elaborately trimmed all around the interior of the brim with flowers, velvet and ribbons framing the face. Around mid-decade the bonnet was lined under the brim with a white frill and the trimmings were often replaced by a tulle cap worn on the head, this cap acquiring a frill towards the end of the decade. In the late 1850s the low-crowned, wide-brimmed sun hat which started to appear in the 1840s gained more acceptance and could be seen in both promenade and carriage outfits. Often made of straw or silk and adorned with ribbons and ostrich feathers, they gave some balance to the huge skirts.

Many hats and bonnets were decorated with flowers. Previously fresh flowers were used, not just in millinery but also to decorate dresses and the hair, often with a tiny vial of water secreted away to keep them fresh. The 1840s and 1850s saw an increasing demand for artificial flowers. In 1855 the World's Fair in Paris gave artificial flower manufacturing a boost with a dedicated stand displaying the likes of tulips, pansies, roses, lilacs, auriculas, primroses and leaves. Made from cambric, muslin, velvet, silks and gauze, dyed to the right hue, the petals and leaves cut to shape and assembled by hand, they were robust and could be used more than once.

Hair in this decade was simply dressed with a centre parting. It could be puffed out over the ears and drawn to a bun or pinned braid at the back. Clusters of curls over the ears were still popular but as the decade progressed the hair was pulled away from the face and ears. 1853 saw a new hairstyle popularised by Eugènie, the new Empress of France. Hair was slightly puffed at the crown and sides, but rolled away form the face revealing the ears and forehead. Indoor caps were still worn by women, but gradually became smaller and were worn further back on the head, decorated with crochet work, lace, embroidery, ribbons and bows or rosettes, or clusters of flowers on each side. Some even had a bavolet like the bonnets.

Until the adoption of the sturdy Balmoral boot, footwear for middle- and upper-class women was relatively insubstantial. They were generally made from soft kid leather or fabric, often with contrasting coloured leather and decorative stitches. For indoors, satin slippers and mules were popular, the latter could be quite beautifully decorated with embroidery, woven fabrics, beaded or even fur lined. In the early years of Victoria's reign there was no left or right shoe, both were identical, straight soled and with the same upper, sometimes marked by the maker with L and R. They would simply take the shape of the foot through wear. Footwear had also gone through a period of being completely flat, but by the mid-1850s heels of an inch or so in height started to appear for both indoor and outdoor use.

Jewellery

Travel for pleasure was a relatively new concept in the Victorian era, with foreign travel having previously been the realm of scholars and the very wealthy. However, the improved communications brought about by the rapidly expanding rail networks and steam ship routes opened the world up to more people. By 1856, Thomas Cook was organising continental railway tours and the resulting interest in foreign countries and cultures and the growth of tourism greatly boosted the international trade in jewellery. As ever, if you had the money, you could purchase beautiful individual hand-crafted pieces, but there was also a profusion of mass produced items specifically for the tourist market.

Popular jewellery included micro-mosaics; first brought back from the Grand Tours of the previous century, these were beautiful brooches, tie pins and decorated boxes created using tiny pieces of coloured glass and depicted sites of Ancient Rome. The ongoing excavations at Pompeii created an interest in cameos carved from lava, and foreign travel also brought pieces made from coral, ivory, tortoiseshell and amber. Naturalism was at the height of its popularity in the 1850s and jewellery often took the form of beautifully modelled branches laden with fruit, flowers and leaves. One of the more unusual materials used till the 1850s was Irish bog oak, this was wood that had been immersed in peat bogs for hundreds of years. It was very dark – almost black – and was hand carved into brooches and pendants for everyday wear, not just for mourning.

Human hair has been used in jewellery for a few hundred years, but it really became an art form in Victorian times. Hair was often used as a memento mori and incorporated into pieces of jewellery to remember a loved one who had passed away; it was more commonly used, however, to commemorate a betrothal or wedding, or simply to create a sentimental piece using hair from a child, a lover, or from a son, husband or father who had left for war. It could be set into rings, brooches (swivel brooches, where one side contained a miniature picture, the other a lock of the loved one's hair were popular), lockets, or even plaited into fobs, bracelets, earrings and necklaces. In short, it became quite a flourishing business in Victorian Britain and when the queen visited Empress Eugénie at Versailles in 1855, she presented her with a bracelet made from her own hair. That same year, at the Paris Exposition, a life-sized portrait of Victoria made entirely of human hair was a very popular exhibit.

Early hair jewellery is often referred to a 'palette' work because the tiny designs were created on an artist's palette then sealed under a crystal cap or in a special compartment in the item. The finest of these brooches were created in the 1840s and throughout the 1850s. Popular designs included Prince of Wales's feathers, tiny landscapes and basket weave patterns. Another technique was called 'table worked hair', where the hair was weighted with bobbins and woven through a special table with a circular hole in the middle in a manner similar to French knitting through a wooden cotton reel. The result was a hollow woven tube used to make bows, rosettes, beads, chains, bracelets with gold or enamel clasps, earrings and so on. In its day it was an attractive novelty, and in comparison to metal jewellery it was extraordinarily light to wear.

For hair to be woven and twisted to create the designs it needed to come from a living person, otherwise it would be too brittle to work. People would leave snippets of their hair to be turned into jewellery once they had died. Adverts in newspapers for hair donors created a fear that the hair you left with a jeweller might not be the hair you got back, consequently ladies would buy instruction books and patterns to create their own jewellery. Following the death of her beloved Albert in 1861, Victoria wore a lock of his hair in a brooch pinned over her heart for the rest of her life.

One of the most popular items of jewellery of the 1850s was the bracelet. Over the decade, bracelets would be worn singly, or with two or more on one arm, and large cabochon stones were popular in both brooches and bracelets. The Victorians love of hidden messages appeared in the form of acrostic jewellery believed to have started in the early 1800s, but it was the Victorians who became the the masters of this. The idea is simple, using the first letter of the gemstone to spell out a hidden message in a ring, pendant or even earrings. An item bearing the word 'love' would contain lapis-lazuli, opal, vermeil (the old name for garnet) and an emerald; for 'dearest' use diamond, emerald, amethyst, ruby, emerald, sapphire and topaz; for 'adore': amethyst, diamond, opal, ruby and emerald. Take a careful look at those antique Victorian pieces that appear to have been made with ill-matched gemstones, they might just contain a hidden message.

The Sewing Machine and Aniline Dyes

In addition to the crinoline cage, two other inventions had a big impact on fashion in the 1850s. The first was the design and patent of the first practical sewing machine by American Isaac Merritt Singer. The sewing machine was nothing new, back in 1829 Barthélemy Thimmonier produced a chain-stitch machine, and in 1832, American William Hunt produced the double-threaded lock-stitch machine. Further improvements were made by other inventors but it was Singer who devised the first machine that could be easily mass produced and would prove to be the most practical for domestic use. In 1855, at the World's Fair in Paris, the Singer brand was awarded first prize, and in the same year Singer became the biggest selling make of sewing machine in the world. A year later he opened his first British high-street shop in Glasgow, the first of many that specialised purely in Singer machines. They could be purchased outright or hired on a weekly basis, and in 1858 Singer introduced the first lightweight domestic machine, the Grasshopper. The hand sewing of clothing was soon to become a labour of the past for many households.

Until the 1850s, ready-made clothing was not easily available. A few enterprising drapers, such as Peter Robinson, did venture into the world of ready-made garments. Robinson was selling completed un-tailored garments such as skirts and mantles by 1856, and his block of shops in London became one of the best known mourning emporiums in the city. Twenty years later he became one of the first to issue a photographic catalogue of his ready-to-wear items. This 'Book of Styles' consisted of a series of carte-de-visites of the outfits with a full description and prices on the back. You can also see newspaper adverts for 'unmade dresses' throughout the Victorian era. These we can assume are garments that are cut out but left to the buyer to put together. The ability to sew was a desired female accomplishment at the time and many women would make smaller items at home such as caps and underwear. Dress fabrics were expensive so the skills of an accomplished dressmaker or seamstress would be employed to make the more technical, fitted garments. There were two types of dressmaker: the 'court dressmaker', who had their own premises comprising of a salon, fitting room and workroom; and the 'private dressmaker' who either received clients in their own home or visited them at theirs.

The introduction of the sewing machine was a boon to dressmakers, but it was essential to the growth of the ready-made market. Until its invention, all clothing was sewn by hand; even though the machines were hand-cranked, they speeded up the sewing process both on a commercial and a domestic level. By the mid-1860s, commercial production of clothing was almost completely done by machine although a certain amount of hand sewing was still required on most garments.

The second big breakthrough in this decade was the discovery of aniline dyes by chemist William Perkin in 1856. Up to this point, dyes were made from natural materials and while there was a large array of colours, they were often not particularly vibrant. Fashion advice was sometimes quite charming; in 1852, *World of Fashion* suggested that when choosing your walking costume, 'should the day be dull [your costume] must harmonise in colour with the day; and the same should the sky be fine and clear, then the colours must be soft, and of light hues.'[16]

Perkin made his discovery by accident when trying to synthesise a man-made replacement for the naturally occurring anti-malarial drug quinine. The by-product of his experiments was a vivid mauve dye, variously called 'Perkins mauve', 'aniline violet' or 'mauveine'. From here were created various shades of purple, magentas, pinks yellows and blues, all of these were far more vivid than any colour available from natural dyes and sporting modern names such as 'acid magenta', 'aldehyde green', 'Verguin's fuchine', 'Martius yellow' and 'Magdela red'. These dyes were cost effective and resistant to fading.

Previously, purple dye had been extremely expensive and clothing of that colour was associated with the clergy and royalty. The reason for the huge cost was because the dye was derived from a certain species of marine snail, and huge numbers of these molluscs would be required to produce the dye – and the colour then faded quickly. Perkin's discovery of the aniline dye would make it it affordable for everyone. Perkin worked hard to publicise his invention, but it was when Queen Victoria and Empress Eugénie were seen in fabric of a similar colour that mauvine became *the* must have fashionable colour for your crinoline, so popular that in 1859 *Punch* referred to the craze as 'Mauve Measels'.

Perkins's discovery sparked a rush to develop more aniline-based dyes. In 1859, French chemists isolated two new purplish dyes, naming both after victories of Napoleon III over the Austrians. The first of these dyes was given the name 'magenta' because it was discovered shortly after the battle of Magenta early in June 1859. The second was named 'solferino' to commemorate the decisive battle of Solferino just twenty days later. In both cases, the colour supposedly represented the appearance of the battlefield after the bloody fighting. Because of its popularity, magenta became known as 'the queen of colours'. Another popular synthetic dye was a vivid green which contained arsenite of copper. After a number of unfortunate and tragic incidents, research and subsequent reports by French and German scientists revealed that the vivid green dye, when used for gloves and clothes, was being absorbed through the skin of the person wearing them with fatal consequences.

With more and more people renting or owning their own sewing machines, and the new and remarkable colours of aniline dyes, a well-stocked draper's shop could usually be found even in quite small towns across the country. Indeed, it would not be unusual for a country market town to support five or more drapery shops, the very best of them in well-appointed premises in the market place, often with impressive signage and frontages proudly displaying their wares in fine window displays and around the door. All of them were very keen to point out that their goods were 'high class,' their staff would be trained to be attentive, and many offered 'easy terms' for those who wished to buy 'on tick' and pay a little off each month.

Fabrics and colours of the 1850s

Some of the most common fabrics and popular colours as recorded in fashion magazines, pattern books and adverts of the 1850s.

Alpaca, barège, bengalene, balzarines, bouracan, broché, Byzantine granité, cambric, camlet, Carmélite, cashmere, crepon, cretonnes, djedda, drap de velour, drap de Venise, droguet, Egyptian cloth, faille (faye), flannel, foulard (checked, spotted, sprigged), French merino, gauze (striped, gold or silver threads, printed), genappe cloth, glacé, grenadine, gros grain (plain,checked), Holland, jacconet, Japanese silk, laine foulard, leno, linen, linsey, longcloth, merino, moiré (antique, embroidered, with satin patterns), mohair (striped, checked, chiné), mousseline de laine, muslin (plain, printed with imitation ruches and pleats), nankin, Ottoman velvet, pekin velvets in broad stripes, percale, plush velvet, poil de chèvre, poplin, poplin de laine with large plaids, poplinette, poplin lama, poplin reps, poult de soie reps with wide vertical stripes, sateen, satin, satin Turc, serge, silk, (plain, striped lengthwise, shot, soyeux linsey, sultane, taffetas (spotted, flowered,chiné), tamatives, tarlatan (plain, striped, sprigged), tulle, turin velvet, tussore, velvet, velveteen, velvet Impératrice, winsey, Azoff green, Bismarck (a plum colour), Bismarck brown, blue, black, blue turc, bois de rose, bright blue, bright rose, brown, bronze-green, buff, cerise, cuir, drab, eau de nil, Eugénie blue, fuschine, garnet, gas green, golden pheasant, green, grenat, grey, Havannah, light blue, magenta, maize, marine blue, mauve, Metternich green, Mexico blue, nacarat (*a light clear red, brilliant as the sun*) neutral tints, Ophelia, orphelian, plaids, plum, purple, ruby-red, scabious, scarlet, solferino, tartans, Vesuvian red, violet, violet blue, white, yellow

Large plaids were popular at the start of the decade as were embroidered poplins (e.g. arabesques or leaves of black velvet), dark colours were preferred for outdoor dress ad the palest hues for evening. In the latter years of the decade it was strong contrasts and striped materials that became very popular.

Mrs E. Kingscote in her 'walking skirt' which has been hitched up, possibly using internal cords, to reveal a coloured petticoat, c.1864.

Chapter 3

1860s

The Romantic Period of Victoria's reign was brought to an abrupt end in 1861 with the unexpected death of her beloved Prince Albert from typhoid fever, aged just 42. The queen, her court and the country went into mourning; for the queen this would last till her death in 1901. The middle era of her reign is often referred to as the Grand or Mid-Victorian Period, which would last till 1885. During this era Britain continued to enjoy prosperity and as the queen took to widow's black, the rest of the country indulged in some of the most ostentatious fashions of the era.

The 1860s Look

Since visual trickery to make the skirts look wider was no longer needed, the flounces of the previous decade disappeared and decoration was often restricted to the lower part of the skirt. Although coloured bands down each seam of the gored skirt could also be found. 'Double' skirts were popular, the lower one often with a deep pleat, flounced or decorated hem, the second skirt, over the top of the first, could be similarly decorated or plain; two different shades of the same material were often used, or even an underskirt of stripes or tartan and a plain overskirt. The loss of the flounces on the skirt meant that a pocket could no longer be secreted away and the reticule became fashionable again, although occasionally there was a small watch pocket at the waist, or even two larger pockets on the front of the skirt. The year 1860 saw the introduction of the 'Isabeau' style dress. This consisted of a bodice and skirt cut in one without a waist seam, which would often sport a row of rosettes or large buttons called 'macarons' from neck to hem.

Around the middle of the decade the fashionable skirt started to change shape. It lost some of its voluminous circumference and the front became flatter; it also became smoother over the hips, with the volume

The 'Isabeau' dress had a bodice and skirt cut in one piece, so it had no waist seam. Characteristically there would be a row of large buttons, called 'macarons' down the front from neck to hem.

At its height of popularity the crinoline could be very wide, here with typical heavy decoration, macron buttons and a beautiful woven shawl, April 1861.

of fabric being gathered up and moving towards the back, often leaving a small train. By the end of the decade the skirt was almost completely flat at the front and draped up at the back and sides, the latter referred to as 'pannier puffs'. The *English Woman's Domestic Magazine* of February 1869, ever the arbiter of the latest fashions, proclaimed: 'the train shaped dress is suitable to wear in the drawing room – not for balls', as the latter requires 'a special toilette, neither short nor cumbersome'. The magazine was quite explicit in its instruction for the wearing of long-trained dresses, they are suitable 'only and exclusively in large parties, and where dancing is out of the question…. To dance a quadrille with a sweeping train is absurd – to waltz with one is frightful.' To wear a full train in a drawing room is deemed objectionable and the wearer is 'to be suspected of misplaced vanity.'[1]

The bodice in the early years of the 1860s was round necked, ending at the natural waistline with a gentle point and fastening at the front. Later, the waist straitened and was often highlighted with a waistband with a small buckle, or on a summer dress a ribbon 'ceinture' with floating ends. A Swiss waist was also popular, worn over the blouse and skirt emphasising the waist. It was a boned and double pointed 'belt' and could be either plain or decorated. Some bodices still had basques, and as the bulk the skirt moved to the back these became shorter in front and longer at the back with inverted pleats.

The pagoda sleeve was losing favour and the most common sleeve became a well-padded, curved bishop sleeve, but from around mid-decade the sleeves narrowed, lost their padding, often developed cuffs and became tight by the end of the decade. Some can be seen with a ribbon bow on the outside of the bend of the arm known as a 'brassard'. Shoulders also dropped and from mid-decade there was emphasis to the top of the sleeves in the form of fringing, braiding or an epaulette. Necklines were generally rounded with a white collar showing which was either a chemisette or a separate collar. Mid- to late-decade saw bodices which have decoration applied to give the look of a squared neckline, the waist of these was usually straight.

Decoration on the skirt and bodice could take the form of pleats, flounces, bands of velvet, geometrical patterns and Greek key designs, florals were not in fashion. Scalloped edges were succeeded by vandykes (shaped like the teeth of a saw) of varying sizes. Other popular trimmings include braiding, fringing, grelots (ball fringe) and ruching. Aniline dyes rapidly became popular, bright primary colour schemes were much admired and there was a vogue for striking contrasting effects mid-decade, contrasting bold trimmings with plain fabrics were very popular. New colours went by names such as Orphelian, Eugénie blue, Azoff Green, bright rose, golden pheasant, Vesuvian red and Bismarck (a plum colour) but the *English Woman's Domestic Magazine* of 1868 recommended that very bright tints should be toned down with trimmings of black, white or grey. Two shades of the same colour were very fashionable although trimmings would be of a contrasting fabric.

One of the most popular colours was Scheele's Green (also known as emerald green or arsenical green), it was used in everything from wallpaper to fabrics, hats, gloves, food dye and paint on children's toys. It was particularly popular in fabrics and wall hangings as the colour preserved its freshness under the new artificial lights. Unfortunately it contained arsenic and was consequently responsible for many deaths. It

The crinoline cage is deflating and sleeves are becoming tighter. The waist here is highlighted by a waistband with a contrasting buckle, c.1867.

The bulk of the skirt is moving to the back, geometrical designs were very popular, particularly on plain fabrics, c.1867.

was used extensively in the production of artificial flowers which were becoming ever more popular; many were made at home by young women who were employed in 'pluffing', whereby they dipped the artificial leaves into warm wax then dusted them with the powdered green colouring. The poisonous powder would be inhaled, get under fingernails, be absorbed into the skin and lodge in clothing. In 1861 an inquest was held into the death of Matilda Scheurer, a 19-year-old artificial-flower maker in London. It was confirmed that she had been slowly poisoned by the inhalation of arsenite of copper used in her work. Tragically, her sister had previously died under the same circumstances.

In 1861, the *Belfast Morning News* ran an article stating that a fashionable lady in a green dress would be surrounded by 92 square feet of fabric, containing about 13 ounces of arsenic. It goes on to explain that a dozen or two such ladies with 'every crush of their dress, every toss of it in a quadrille' would be giving off poisonous arsenic dust. Prolonged contact with the arsenic powder could produce many symptoms, such as headache, thirst, loss of appetite, sickness, diarrhoea, sore throat and gums, swelling about the eyes, sore and running nose and open sores. Thankfully, by the end of the century Scheele's Green had become obsolete after it had been been replaced by safer dyes.

A popular fashion early in the decade was the Garibaldi blouse, named after the Italian General Guiseppe Garibaldi and his famous red shirts. It was high necked with full sleeves gathered into a tight cuff and was popular for the first half of the decade for casual wear, on holiday or relaxing at home. Traditionally, the blouse was scarlet with black braid and buttons, but was also available in black and paler fabrics. It was often worn with a Swiss waist or belt and under a Zouave jacket. Taking its name from a similar garment worn by Algerian troops, this was a short, cropped, open jacket with no collar, curved front pieces, fastening at the throat only. It was often made of scarlet wool and had long loose-fitting sleeves which could be cut open to the elbow, and it was often decorated with gold or black soutache braid or black and white stitching.

With the growth in popularity of outdoor pursuits for ladies such as walking, croquet, archery and days at the seaside, it became obvious that the crinoline was not particularly conducive to a more active lifestyle and a clever compromise was developed. The 'walking skirt' was ankle-length, or was designed so that the bottom could be raised to around about ankle height. This was achieved using internal cords which pulled the hem to the desired height. Another version had tabs at intervals around the underside of the hem which would button onto the outside of the skirt, thus looping it up. Once raised it exposed the petticoat which would often be striped or coloured.

Bathing costumes were becoming both more popular and acceptable in the 1860s, but mixed bathing was still not tolerated on most public beaches. In 1866 the bathing outfit for women consisted of a full bodice

Another walking ensemble, complete with walking pole, taken in Grasmere in the Lake District.

with short sleeves and an attached skirt buttoning down the front and reaching to the knee, underneath were ankle-length trousers; a linen cap on the head, and on the feet flat pumps with ribbons round the ankles. These sporting outfits were usually made from stronger materials such as stout cottons, linens, serge and wools, although flannel was avoided for bathing costumes as it would become waterlogged.

Punch, as ever, was keen to highlight the more 'outlandish' fashions and in 1860 published a poem which was reprinted in newspapers throughout the country, entitled Fast Young Ladies. The second verse reads:

> Wide awake our heads adorn,
> Fast young ladies;
> Feathers in our hats are worn,
> Fast young ladies;
> Skirts hitched up on spreading frame,
> Dandy high-heeled boots, proclaim
> Fast young ladies.

Foundation Garments

The crinoline cage was at the peak of its popularity in the late 1850s and early 1860s when it reached its most epic proportions of up to 6 yards circumference. Most women kept it to a more sensible size but this did not prevent it becoming a target for satirical humour in newspapers and periodicals. It was was embraced by women at all levels of society, the *Wells Journal* would ruminate:

Fashion has turned the brain of all society, peeresses at court, queens on their thrones, actresses on stage, and even servants in the waiting room and kitchen, feel that they would be unworthy to rank with humanity were they not to swell out with crinoline to the dimensions of a moderately sized mountain. By the extension of their dresses they make everything incongruous and out of place. To enter the widest door they require compression, to obtain a seat in an omnibus the assistance of three or four gentlemen is necessary, and any gentleman who may essay to do the gallant for two young ladies, finds himself most ingloriously buried amidst folds of silk or muslin.[2]

As with every new fashion item the newspapers carried many adverts for the new crinoline cage. W.S. & E.H. Thompson & Co of Cheapside were the leading manufacturer of 'skeleton petticoats', the London factory produced 4,000 a day in the 1860s and employed over 1,000 women. Their Thompson Patent Crown Crinoline was considered to be one of the best after winning a prize medal for crinolines at the International Exhibition and advertising for it would unashamedly boast that 'the ordinary weight of stuff petticoats exceeds two pounds, but the new cage petticoat is not more than half a pound, which gives them a great advantage in a hygienic sense'.[3]

Another make was the 'Patent Ondina, or Waved Jupon' which advertised that it,

> does away with the unsightly results of the ordinary hoops, and so perfect are the wave-like bands that a lady may ascend a steep stair, lean against a table, throw herself into an arm-chair, pass to her stall at the opera, or occupy a fourth seat in a carriage without inconveniences to herself or others, or provoking the rude remarks of the observers ... .Prices 18s. 6D, 21s. & 25s 6d[4]

There was also the 'Patent Gutta Percha Crinoline as advertised in the *Glasgow Herald* as 'a great curiosity', it was described as:

> vulcanised with Gutta Percha [a form of naturally occurring latex, classified in 1843] quite light, not the slightest smell; can bear a good squeeze without getting out of order. Ladies that have worn them say they are very comfortable and durable, and can be kept perfectly clean by means of a wet sponge.[5]

The *Leicester Journal* of February 1864 included an article from *Railway News* which illustrates the size of the crinoline cage industry at its height, pointing to:

> Not less than 100 tons of crinoline steel are carried over the Manchester, Sheffield, and Lincolnshire Railway weekly. Sheffield is the principle seat of the manufacture; the fabrication of this delicate article giving employment to a large number of its population. Taking

the average weight of each set of crinoline steel hoops at half a pound, the above quantity of steel shows a production of about half a million of crinoline per week, independent of what passes from Sheffield by other routes. The quantity of steel hoops thus manufactured weekly to enlarge the seeming proportions of the fair sex, if joined together in a continuous wire would almost compass the globe.[6]

With the expansion in skirt width came an increase in accidents associated with the vast amount of fabric, particularly those involving fire. At a time when naked flames were everywhere, expansive skirts were simply accidents waiting to happen. Injury and death caused by clothes catching fire was nothing new, one of the most famous cases being that of Clara Webster. In December 1844 while dancing the role of Zelika, a royal slave in the Revolt of the Harem in Drury Lane, her gauzy skirt brushed one of the open gas jets lighting the stage. Her outfit was quickly alight, and she suffered severe burns, dying three days later aged only 21. The inquest found that the accident could have been avoided by the simple acts of putting a wire guard over the naked flames and by fireproofing costumes. Fabrics could easily be made flame retardant using a solution of alum, or nitrate of ammonia. However, dancers were reluctant to do this as the process not only discoloured the fabrics but also stiffened them, making outfits uncomfortable and causing them to lose the floaty etherealness that was often desired.

By the early 1860s the number of deaths caused by such accidents had increased and every week there would be stories recorded in the papers of fatal incidents. In January 1861 Miss E. Power, aged 31, reached up to straighten a candle on the mantle shelf, her skirt brushed the fire and ignited. At the inquest the coroner stated that the crinoline had kept the flames from the lower part of her body remarking that it was both 'the bane

A very fashionable striped dress, note the less padded sleeves ending in cuffs and the decorative scalloped edge, c1867.

and the antidote'.[7] This was not the case in all accidents though, the lack of protective layers of petticoats often meant the victim was badly burned. *The Examiner* of 4 January 1862 reported four fatal accidents, the youngest being 14-year-old Sarah Wainwright whose dress caught fire at the grate while she was alone. There are no exact numbers available regarding deaths caused by crinoline fires, but it is estimated to be about 3,000 between the late 1850s and late 1860s. In 1863–64 alone, Florence Nightingale estimated that at least 630 women had died from fatal dress accidents.

With the crinoline being the preferred fashion for all levels of society, accidents also occurred in workplaces. The *Cork Examiner* in June 1864 records the death of Ann Rollinson from injuries sustained when her crinoline was caught in revolving machinery in a mangling room at Firwood bleach works. Thankfully, not all workplace accidents were fatal, the *Newcastle Journal* reports:

> The inconveniences of crinoline have been found so great in the Staffordshire Potteries, that the principal manufacturers, Messrs. Copeland, Messrs. Minton and others, have forbidden the use of crinolines on their premises during the hours of work. In one shop alone, the losses by breakage of articles swept down by them amounted to £200 a year. The workshops became too small, and the work was impeded.[8]

Women would generally have two cages, one for the daytime and one for the evening/night-time; it was considered indispensable for all activities, with the exception of horse riding. However, the cage itself was not without its dangers, the *English Woman's Domestic Magazine* in October 1862 recommended that the bottom 18 inches of the crinoline cage be covered inside and out with fabric to prevent the foot accidentally catching in the steel loops and tripping the wearer. Making this cover removable also allowed the hem, the most likely area to pick up dirt and experience wear and tear, to be cleaned and repaired. Beneath the crinoline would be worn a short petticoat, in cold weather this would be made from wool or flannel; over the top of the cage one or two petticoats of fabrics such as cotton, flannel or camlet, a wool/cotton mix.

The fact that the crinoline cage was affordable and worn by all levels of society was one of the reasons the upper classes started to abandon it mid-decade, and its sheer inconvenience did not endear it to anyone after a while. The bulk of the skirt started to move to the back and as the skirt changed in shape so the crinoline cage shrank to become the half-crinoline or 'crinolette'. These were long petticoats that had steels only in the back half, the front being simply a fabric flat drape curving upwards, leaving the knees and lower legs exposed. In addition to the lower steels there were others inserted into the top of the petticoat, angled diagonally and, using internal tapes, pulled into half hoops to support the excess fabric now at the back of the skirt.

Some crinolettes had internal tapes for the lower steels too, allowing the shape of the petticoat and thus the skirt to be changed. The crinolette was the mid-point between the full crinoline cage and the bustle, and is variously known as the 'tournure' or bustle/dress improver in Britain. As the weight of the skirts moved to the back rather than being evenly spread about the person, women tended to develop what was called the 'Grecian bend'. The weight at the back caused a natural tendency to lean forward to compensate, this was exacerbated by the high heels and corset: 'However superb or simple a lady's costume may be, it is mainly dependent for its elegance of adjustment and distinctiveness of style to the corset and crinoline beneath it.'[9]

By the mid-1860s corsets were shorter and the fashion for a higher more rounded look meant they fitted across the bust with boning to give the bosom a gentle nudge upwards, a look which could be enhanced by inserting small woollen pads into the bodice lining. The corset panels were boned, quilted or corded to control the waist and stomach, and the hip area was curved but not boned, giving the hips a rounded shape in line with the crinoline, some even sported a quilted roll at the bottom to help support the weight and shape of the crinoline cage.

The overall shape was the famous 'hourglass', although the huge skirts made waists look smaller without corsets being tightly laced. The new bright dyes found their way into corsets as women wanted something more modern than the usual neutral colours. Corsets were now made from separate pieces that were curved to follow the contours of the body and in the late 1860s steam moulding was introduced to give them a curvier shape. This process saw the completed corsets starched, dried, then stiffened by being placed on a shaped steam mould, thus 'setting' their desired shape. Corset-making was big business, in 1868 William Barry Lord recorded that the corset makers in London employed 10,000, while provincial firms had a further 25,000 workers. Cheap ready-made corsets were also widely available but were a false economy because the use of cheaper materials often led to the busk shattering, potentially causing injury.

Under the corset the chemise was generally still a voluminous, round necked garment hanging down to the calves, although on occasion stopping at the knees. The addition of tucks, lace, openwork and embroidery to underwear turned them into garments that were becoming attractive rather than merely functional. However, the *Englishwoman's Domestic Magazine* complained that 'the amount of embroidery put upon underclothing nowadays is sinful; a young lady spent a month in hem stitching and embroidering a garment which it was scarcely possible that any other human being, except her laundress, would ever see.'[10]

No such frivolity would be seen on the flannel under vests and merino vests (long or short sleeved) advertised in 1867, these were simply warm and functional.

Accessories

Enormous skirts needed appropriate outdoor wear and the shawl was still a popular choice, with those from India being a particular favourite. There were plain ones made from camel's wool, Decca shawls were silk with a black background and large patterns in bright colours, and Delhi shawls had plain backgrounds decorated with raised coloured embroidery. A good alternative to the shawl was the long loose-fitting mantles; a very loose-fitting jacket with either wide sleeves or armhole slits, it produced an almost triangular silhouette.

In the early 1860s the bonnet grew narrower and rose at the front with a 'spoon' shaped brim filled with the usual array of trimmings such as flowers, fruit, ribbons and lace, but this had collapsed by the middle years of the decade and then began to shrink in size. Bonnets remained popular but as the decade progressed, hats were becoming more widely accepted, though you would be frowned up on for wearing one to church on a Sunday. Like the bonnets, hats were decorated with all manner of things from feathers to fringing, flowers to small birds, and both bonnets and hats could be seen with long ribbon streamers known as 'follow-me-lads'. There were a number of styles of hat seen during the decade, the Marie

A simple cloak was popular, giving the typical triangular silhouette of the era. Note the underside of the bonnet is filled with decoration, c.1863.

Shawls were popular and easy to wear with the crinoline. Hats became more acceptable for everyday wear and because the ears are now exposed, earrings became fashionable, c.1862.

Antoinette had a low crown with a wider brim slightly turned up at the sides and down at the front and back; the 'bergère' was oval with a low crown and turned down brim; mid-decade there was a brief fashion for the Scottish Glengarry.

At the start of the 1860s hair had a central parting, with volume over the ears and pulled back into a low chignon which was often enclosed in a chenille hairnet. Sometimes side curls were pinned to the side of the head, or a narrow plait looped down around the ear and back into the chignon. Occasionally, a small pill-box style hat with a turned-up brim lying almost flush with the crown, usually in black velvet and trimmed with feathers was worn. An alternative was to have the hair combed back, with two long curls hanging down at the back and pulled over the shoulders. Gradually the low chignon (which could be a mixture of real and false hair) moved up the head towards the crown, pushing diminishing hats forward onto the forehead as 1870 drew nearer. Mid-

Hair had a central parting with volume over the ears and was often enclosed in a chenille hairnet. Note the pockets on the front of the skirt, c.1861.

This lady is wearing a wide sleeved mantle and carrying the newly fashionable straw hat, c1862.

decade saw the fullness at the temples waved then pulled back to reveal the ears, the hair then pulled back to a low, loose knot at the back. Indoor caps were still worn but were smaller, resting on top of the head with streamers hanging at the back.

The chignon could consist of curls, plaits or a simply coiled loop, but not all women could grow enough hair to create a large chignon. All was not lost, however, as there was a healthy trade in hair pieces, made from human hair. *The Times* reported that Marseilles was the main centre for the trade in human hair, importing 40,000 lbs annually and goes on to explain that 'the weight of hair in an ordinary chignon does not exceed three ounces and a half, the annual quantity imported into Marseilles alone would be sufficient for upwards of 180,000 headdresses.'[11]

The fashion for false hair would, like the skirts of the 1860s, reach epic proportions in the 1870s.

As the hair moved up the ears became exposed and larger earrings came into fashion. There was a general vogue throughout the decade for heavy, large pieces of jewellery, brooches, large necklaces with large pendants and wide bracelets with buckles were all popular and can often be seen in photographs. But you may also see a very long delicate chain draped over the bodice, sometimes looped onto a brooch or into the waistband or simply worn full-length. These are known as guard chains and were about 60 inches (153cm) long, as well as being simply for decoration, they could also be used to carry a watch or lorgnettes. If the former it would be tucked into the watch pocket at the waist. Silver became popular as did the delicate item of jewellery known as the Patti jets, a ball of polished jet hanging from a ribbon necklace and worn with matching earrings. Not all jet, or even black jewellery, was for mourning purposes; it was in fact quite fashionable.

The introduction of the crinoline cage meant that once again ladies' feet would, on the swing of the cage, be on display. Consequently, coloured footwear and stockings became popular, in some of the new bright aniline dyes. Stockings were made from silk, wool and cotton and white ones were generally worn with shoes, but with boots colours such as scarlet, green and mauve were worn with plaid, vertical and horizontal stripes coming into fashion by the end of the decade. The heels of the 1850s continued into this decade and by the early 1860s also started to appear on boots as well as shoes. Mid-decade, toes started to become more rounded and decorations on boots such as tassels were found. The elastic-sided boot was still a popular choice but both the buttoned and lace-up boot were still being worn.

Fabrics and colours of the 1860s

Listed below are some of the most common fabrics and popular colours as recorded in fashion magazines, pattern books and adverts of the 1860s. At the start of the decade it was not just colours but large plaids that were popular. Through the decade, it was a time when the most fashionable outfits had strong contrasts and striped materials. Silk was particularly popular as it took the aniline dyes very well and had a glossy sheen.

Alpaca, barège, bengalene, balzarines, bouracan, broché, Byzantine granité, cambric, camlet, cashmere, crepon, cretonnes, djedda, drap de velour, drap de Venise, droguet, Egyptian cloth, faille (faye), flannel, foulard (checked, spotted, sprigged), French merino, gauze (striped, gold or silver threads, printed), genappe cloth, glacé, grenadine, gros grain (plain, checked), Holland, jacconet, Japanese silk, laine foulard, leno, linen, linsey, longcloth, merino, moiré (antique, embroidered, with satin patterns), mohair (striped, checked, chiné), mousseline de laine, muslin (plain, printed with imitation ruches and pleats), nankin, Ottoman velvet, pekin velvets in broad stripes, percale, plush velvet, poil de chèvre, poplin, poplin de laine with large plaids, poplinette, poplin lama, poplin reps, poult de soie reps with wide vertical stripes, sateen, satin, satin Turc, serge, silk, (plain, striped lengthwise, shot, jacquard) soyeux linsey, sultane, taffetas (spotted, flowered,chiné), tamatives, tarlatan (plain, striped, sprigged), tulle, turin velvet, tussore, velvet, velveteen, velvet Impératrice, winsey.

Acid Magenta, aldehyde green, Azoff green, Bismarck (a plum colour), Bismarck brown, blue, black, blue turc, bois de rose, bright blue, bright rose, brown, bronze-green, buff, cerise, claret, cuir, drab, eau de nil, Eugénie blue, fuschine, garnet, gas green, golden pheasant, green, grenat, grey, Havannah, lighth blue, magdela red, magenta, maize, marine blue, martius yellow, mauve, Metternich green, Mexico blue, neutral tints, Ophelia, orphelian, plaids, plum, purple, ruby-red, cabious, scarlet, solferino, tartans, Verguins fuchsine, Vesuvian red, violet, violet blue, white, yellow.

This beautiful velvet dress is unusual in its lack of decoration. The plait on the head is likely to be false, c.1875.

Chapter 4

1870s

The earlier years of Victoria's reign had seen the skirt take on either a bell or dome shape, then changed again through the 1860s with the emphasis moving to the back of the costume. The new decade of the 1870s saw a slimmer silhouette gradually start to dominate, but not before clothing reached a peak of elaborate trimmings, and hairstyles became the largest and most complex they would ever be. The press, ever keen to mock, took stock of the extremes of female fashion to date in a piece that appeared in a number of newspapers in 1873. Entitled 'Recipe to Make a Fashionable Woman' it suggested:

Take ninety-nine pounds of flesh and bones – but chiefly bones – bore holes in the ears, cut off the small toes; bend the back to conform to the Grecian Bend, the Boston Dip, the kangaroo Droop, or the Saratoga Slope, as the taste inclines; then add three yards of linen, one hundred yards of ruffles, seventy-five yards of edging, eighteen yards of ruffles, seventy-five yards of edging, eighteen yards of dimity, one pair of silk or cotton hose, six yards of flannel, embroidered, one pair of Balmoral boots with heels three inches high, four pounds of whalebone in strips, two hundred and sixty yards of steel wire, half a mile of tape, two pounds of cotton or wire hemispheres, fifty yards of silk or other dress goods, one hundred yards of point lace, four hundred yards of fringe and other trimmings, twelve gross of buttons, one box of pearl powder, one saucer of carmine, one bushel of 'store' hair, frizzled and fretted a al maniaque, one quart of hair pins, one pound of braid, one lace handkerchief nine inches square, with patent holder, perfumed with attar of roses and musk.[1]

The 'Kangaroo Droop' mentioned in the piece was a brief fashion fad of the early 1870s described as:

a glove with three or four buttons is selected so that the wrist may be as long and as small as possible. The wrist of the left hand, and also that of the right hand if it is not engaged with an Alpine parasol, is brought close to the breast, and then the hand is permitted to fall, palm downward, as if all muscular action were lost ... and suggests the loveliest helplessness imaginable.[2]

The 'Boston Dip', also a fad of the early 1870s, was simply a false limp on the leading foot as though you have a painful heel.

Although exaggerated to some extent, it is interesting to see the vagaries of fashion summarised like this, and it should be remembered that this was written prior to the excessive use of false hair and overabundance of trimmings of the 1870s. The following two decades would have their own distinctive, and some would say outlandish, fashions, but nothing like the excessive use of false hair and ornamentation the 1870s indulged in.

The 1870s Look

By the time 1870 dawned the fullness of the skirt had settled high up at the rear in what is known as the 'early bustle' style, which lasted from 1869 to 1876. Supported by a combination of the crinolette and interior tapes tied together, which helped give the skirt the bouffant shape at the back, the front was now almost flat. Separate drapes could be worn like an apron over the front of the underskirt, it could lie flat or be gathered up at the sides. Similarly a 'double skirt' was a popular look, shorter than the underskirt and worn over the top, this overskirt produced an apron-like front, and could be ruched up at the sides, with the back puffed up over the bustle. The apron could be pointed or round, the back edges flat, rounded, square or pointed – in fact the edges could be designed to give a variety of looks, but this, along with the skirt and bodice, was heavily decorated with pleats, flounces, braid, tucks, lace, ribbon, fringing and ruching, in various combinations. At times there was nothing subtle about the decorative trimmings on an outfit, nor the jewellery that was worn. Very large, heavy necklaces, chains and pendants became popular, especially in jet, and often more than one was worn. Big bracelets were also worn, sometimes on both wrists, and silver became very popular, as well as the large expensive pieces, smaller die-stamped brooches and other items could now be mass produced, making them affordable for many.

The bodice was close fitting and short, giving it a higher than natural waistline, and would have rounded, square or 'V' neckline, the latter could be filled with a high-necked blouse or chemisette. Higher necklines could be trimmed 'en carré', meaning the decoration simulated a low square neckline, or 'en pelerine' to simulate a small shoulder cape. They were often decorated with frills, braid, bows and other trims. Some bodices had two points in front and behind but mostly they had a basque falling below the waist, the edges of which could be pointed, square or rounded

The overskirt is draped at the front and ruched at the sides and back to produce the bustle, c.1875.

and those at the back sat on top of the bustle like coat tails; this combined with the overskirt gave a layered look. A jacket-style bodice was trimmed to look like an open jacket over a waistcoat using trims and different fabrics. Sleeves began below the shoulder-line, and during the first years of the new decade the wide pagoda sleeves of the 1860s could still be seen, gradually becoming more fitted with decorative cuffs and buttons.

The early 1870s brought the polonaise, a refashioning of an eighteenth-century garment, it consisted of a tight bodice and long skirt in one and was usually made from a fabric different to that of the skirt. The bodice generally had a square neckline and the attached skirts could either be worn loose or be looped up and draped in a fashion displaying a decorative underskirt. Sleeves were long and fitted with a cuff, or with pagoda or Marie Antoinette sleeves in summer. After the death of Charles Dickens in June 1870 there was a brief vogue for the 'Dolly Varden' polonaise, named after his heroine in Barnaby Rudge, this was made of chintz and was worn over a brightly coloured skirt, often with either a large bow or two large buttons at the back of the waist.

The bodice is short and high fitting, the V-neckline is filled with a chemisette and is decorated 'en pelerine' to simulate a small shoulder cape, c.1871.

These young sisters wear a contrasting overskirt pulled up at the back to form the bustle, the pagoda sleeves could still be seen early in the decade, c.1873.

The one-piece 'princess line' dress, named after Alexandra, Princess of Wales, whose wearing of the style popularised this new look in the mid-1870s, had no horizontal waist seam, instead the long, slender silhouette was created by extended boning and vertical tucks and darts, buttoning down the front that created the appearance of extending the torso. The dress could have an inserted front panel that was wider at the neck, narrowing as it got to the waist and carried on below, creating a slimming effect.

Similarly, the cuirass bodice, named after a piece of armour, also became very popular from around 1874. It was tight-fitting, shaped and heavily boned on all seams, forming a smooth unbroken line reaching below the hips. The cuirass was generally made from a different material to the drapes and skirt and was fastened down the front, had a high neck and tight sleeves, its length forcing the bustle downwards. The back of the cuirass was fitted and narrow, the shoulder seams now sitting behind the shoulders. It was popular to have this made in two shades of the same colour with the bodice and skirt being pale and the centre-front and centre-back panels darker. The darker shade could be repeated on the skirt trimmings. By the late 1870s and into the early 1880s the cuirass is seen to be cut higher over the hips but dipping to a point front and back. The fashion for a narrow vertical line was emphasised by the clever use of contrasting materials of the same colour, such as silk and velvet or wool and velvet, long pleats and trimmings.

One innovation that aided the manufacture of tight-fitting cuirass bodices was the production of woven wool or silk stretch fabrics. It was the development of circular knitting machines producing tubes of fabric that could then be cut and sewn to create a bodice that ushered in this daring fashion for those that wanted show their figure to its fullest advantage. The Jersey Costume, as it was called, was not favoured by all, the *Daily Review* reported:

An aristocratic drawing room was lately scandalised by the appearance of a fashionable lady garbed in a cream-coloured jersey reaching below the knees, where it finishes under drapery, the only relief to the rather too sharply outlined figure. Undoubtedly such a statuesque display is to be guarded against, but the veriest prude could freely adopt the fashion if modified according to the plan of leading dressmakers, and made as for the Princess of Wales.

To obtain this result, accurate measures are sent to the manufacturer, who weaves an elastic silk vest of graceful shape, with open stocking seams replacing the single front gores and the seams under the arms. The bodice next passes into the hands of the couturiere, who binds with silk the neck, armholes, and sides of the back, stiffening the latter by whalebones, along which runs a close set of eyelet holes. Then are added sleeves in silk, satin or velvet always matching the skirt, as well as the military collar, clasped by a silver necklet. As a good substitute a lace ruffle is often employed. The lower edge of the jersey is hidden beneath a scarf, as from a distance it has merely the appearance of an exquisitely moulded satin cuirass.[3]

Despite the likes of Lily Langtry and Princess Alexandra favouring the garment it was not always popular at formal occasions and had a fairly short life. Another reason for this may be that, because of the way it was manufactured and the fact it stretched, there was no fastening and the wearer had to wriggle into it. Not so much of an issue if it was to be worn all day, but etiquette dictated regular changes of clothing and pulling the jersey on and off over carefully styled hair was not very convenient.

Punch, as ever, had something to say about the fashion,

> Then she wore a jersey fitting
> Like an eel skin all complete,
> With a skirt so tight that sitting
> Was an agonising feat.

The jersey was, however, considered a little more appropriate for lawn tennis and soirees for which 'delicate shades, both plain and striped'[4] were reserved. For sporting events it was usually teamed with a serge or flannel skirt. However, despite an increasing popularity of sporting activities for women it was not always deemed appropriate if you cared about your appearance. *Sylvia's Home Journal* compared a woman taking part in a lawn tennis competition rather unflatteringly 'to a swan waddling on a bowling green, for women clad in the dresses of the present day were never intended by Providence to run.'[5]

A young woman sporting the daring 'Jersey Costume' of tubular knitted fabric and an unusually short hair style, 1880.

Around the middle of the decade the silhouette began to change again, the natural waist reappeared, the shoulder-line lifted, sleeves tightened, the V-neck vanished and the bustle slipped down the back, losing its bouffant fullness. Buttons were either centre front or centre back, and silk dresses often laced at the back. The tightening of the bodice meant that sleeves also needed to become quite narrow, they were often made of a different material or colour to the bodice which further emphasised the slim look. The fullness in the skirt was now drawn behind in pleats below the hips, sometimes as low down as the knees, held in potion by internal tapes which drew the fabric close to the front of the legs; this was known as the 'tie back' dress or, more fashionably, the 'fourreau' (French for sheath).

The new fashion hugged the figure so closely that it became known as the 'Natural Form' era, although it was short lived, lasting only about five years. Often there was a heavy train at the back supported by a demi-petticoat or stiffened muslin and decorated with pleats and frills. The front of the skirt narrowed giving a sheath like appearance and was often draped, or gathered horizontally, giving the impression it was wrapped around the legs. Late in the decade the lower section of the skirt could involve long pleats, again emphasising the vertical look. Various fabrics could be used on one dress, either the same or a contrasting colour, a darker shade being used for the centre-front and centre-back panels of the bodice, increasing the illusion of slimness. The addition of a pocket on the front was popular. The *Ladies Treasury* bemoaned that 'our skirts are now so tight that our sitting and walking are seriously inconvenienced'.[6] This new sheath-like look would continue for the rest of the decade.

One item of clothing gaining in popularity in the late 1870s – in complete contrast to the fitted look – was the Tea Gown. Ladies, including the Princess of Wales, started wearing them in their boudoir among female friends when drinking tea around about 5 o'clock in the afternoon. Described as 'a charming déshabillé, which is made of costly material and scarce design, and of such an easy, clinging, flowing sweep that visions of Pompeian beauties, gorgeous Cleopatras, or laughing Nell Gwynnes float before the enchanted imagination'.[7] They were frothy concoctions of light fabrics, lace and ribbons, one is described as being made in ruby surah, lavishly trimmed with Breton lace and straw-coloured bows. Maybe they provided an hour or so respite from the constrictions of fashion before a lady had to don her gown for dinner, their popularity certainly carried on into the next decade, despite moralists accusing them of promoting free and easy manners.

Alexandra, Princess of Wales

With the death of Prince Albert in 1861, Victoria consigned herself to a life of mourning and her influence on the world of fashion faded. So when in 1863, at the age of 18, Princess Alexandra of Denmark married Prince Albert Edward, the eldest son of Queen Victoria, the eyes of the English newspapers were on her. At 18 years old she was the same age as Victoria had been when she ascended the throne, but unlike Victoria she was tall, slim, and was also considered to be very beautiful. Newspapers reported that her wedding dress consisted of:

> a petticoat of pearl-white silk, embroidered with the rose, thistle and shamrock, trimmed with four rows of silver lace round the bottom, robing up the centre, over which will be suspended a train of crimson velvet, magnificently embroidered with the same designs as the silver petticoat. The bodice and sleeves are composed of the same costly material.[8]

The newlywed prince and princess of Wales were, without doubt, the toast of London society.

This decade would also see the height of carte de visite 'cartomania'. Not only did people collect photographs of friends and family, they also bought carte de visite of current figures in the press, including the royal family, especially the princess of Wales, and her style was both scrutinised and copied as a result.

Princess Alexandra was young and very popular with the British people. She was not only keen to keep up with the latest trends in style, colour and fabric, but she was also adept at dressing in a manner befitting her status, accentuating her best features and hiding perceived physical flaws. To hide a scar on her neck she wore day dresses with high collars, and for the evening replaced the high collar with multiple layers of pearl and diamond necklaces which became known as a 'collier de chien', or dog collar. This look became particularly popular with society ladies.

The princess also sparked a somewhat strange fashion called the 'Alexandra Limp'. After a bout of rheumatic fever in 1867, Princess Alexandra walked with a slight limp for a number of years. The fashion conscious of the time, admiring everything about the princess, followed suit. The newspapers announced that the 'Alexandra Limp' 'threatens to supersede chignons, paniers, wasp-waists, and the Grecian bend',[9] and would even report, in all seriousness:

Shoemakers in London now offer their fair customers the choice of boots with equally high heels for each foot, or the far more charming variety of a high heel for one foot and a low heel for the other, causing the wearer to halt in a way supposed to be imitative of Royalty.[10]

These mismatched boots were complimented by the use of a cane or walking stick. Thankfully, this strange trend did not last too long, vanishing as the skirts narrowed mid-decade and women were forced to take smaller steps. Princess Alexandra's influence did not end there, the Princess Line dress, first introduced by Charles Frederick Worth, was named after her and indeed her tall slim figure was displayed to perfection in it, doing much to popularise the style. Later in the decade her short curly fringe and tight chignons became the fashion must-have.

Foundation Garments

Initially there was little change to underwear in general apart from an increasing use of colour, particularly in corsetry. Skirts were still shaped by the crinolette, initially worn at the small at the back but gradually slipping to the base of the spine, giving the fashionable softly curved look. Petticoats were worn both over and under the crinolette and in line with the skirts; the fronts could be smooth but the back could carry rows of ruffles right up to the waist, heavily starched to help hold up the skirt.

Fabrics were often muslins, silk, satins or merino for colder weather, although 1877 saw adverts for 'chamois leather petticoats and vests'.[11] and there is also reference to 'chamois leather drawers'.[12] It was in this decade that the bustle, separated from the crinolette to become an item in its own right. As the skirt deflated there was no need for the crinolette, the bustle could provide all the uplift needed until it vanished completely for a short while c.1878–82, during the Natural Form era. Spring 1874 saw an adverts appear for the 'Duplex Crinolette. Lying against, instead of encircling, the figure. No steels in front.' The same advert sees a depiction of the 'Corymbus Bustle, the novelty of the season. Made of Chinese straw plaits, without steel.' And the 'Rouleau Panier, a novelty in form and principle. Light elegant and effective.'[13]

The latter two items are small, not reaching much below the bottom, and are made from two completely different materials, straw and wire,

The 'princess line' dress, long and slender with no waist seam and buttons down the front. Note the chain and small watch pocket, c.1876.

Note the clever addition of velvet panels to give the impression of reveres and the illusion of a slimmer waist, c1876.

the Corymbus bustle being a simple arched wire cage. The bustle could also take the form of a ribbed and/or frilled cushion made from crinoline, colourful cotton, and flannel and could be stuffed with anything from horsehair to down to retain their shape and give form to the dress.

The move from huge skirts and non-fitted bodices to the new long, slimline look meant that there was, quite literally, no room for the somewhat voluminous underwear previously worn. Too much fabric round the bust and hips from the chemise would cause unsightly wrinkles. The bunching of the chemise fabric and the gathered drawstring waist of the drawers under the tighter corset would prove to be both bulky and uncomfortable. One way to relieve this was to shape the chemise between the bust and waist, adding bust seams and removing the extra fabric. However, it was the design of a one-piece garment in c.1877 that provided the real solution. These 'combinations' were simply a garment that combined the chemise and drawers in one. Buttoning down the front, the inside leg seam was left open. They would be made from lightweight cotton fabrics in such lawn, batiste or muslin, although for additional warmth, merino or lambs' wool could be used.

At the same time that the chemise was adapting to the new tightly fitting outfits, the corset also had to evolve. Emphasis was now on a smooth defined bust, slim waist and smooth hips, and the corset had to change to achieve this. The previous, shorter corset with an unboned flare at the hip was replaced by a longer-line garment that extended over the hips and was more heavily boned from top to bottom, and with the loss of the crinoline, tighter lacing came back into fashion. The slim look was aided by the invention in the late 1870s of the spoon busk; as its name implies, rather than being straight, this busk expanded out at the bottom in a dish shape. This allowed the corset to be pulled tighter, reducing the waist size further without producing a bulge at the bottom – that squeezed flesh has to go somewhere. The spoon busk effectively compressed and controlled the abdomen, reducing the unsightly bulge. It was claimed that it was far less harmful to the wearer as it spread the pressure over the abdomen while still achieving the desired smooth, flat look. As with much of the garment industry, the sewing machine was now employed in the manufacture of the corset, machines were also devised that could do the reinforced flossing over the ends of the boning channels.

Despite the narrowing of the silhouette with the arrival of the princess dress, petticoats were still worn. The princess petticoat, like the combinations, was a combined garment designed to reduce bulk. Incorporating a camisole and petticoat, there was no waist seam and the bodice was close fitting. As the bulk of the skirt moved to the back, so did the bulk of the petticoat. Controlled by horizontal drawstrings across the back half, one just below the knee, the other about ankle-length, the width could be adjusted to suit the skirt. An article in the *Cheltenham Chronicle* regarding winter petticoats explained that 'to secure their perfect fit, they are provided, like dresses, with strings and elastics, and many fasten on the sides,' and goes on to describe one such petticoat as:

pale blue flannel terminated by a six inch flounce wrought with silk of two shades; beneath it projects a muslin pleating finished with blue Torchon. These elegant flannel skirts are generally worn with upper ones of foulard – blue, rose, grey, pale yellow, and white being prevailing tints. They take from seven to ten yards, according to the width of their three flounces, the lowermost pleated the top frilling gathered, and measuring twice the circumference of the hem. Either pinking out, embroidery, or festoons finish them off, the scallops giving most support, and no trimming is complete without an under pleating of lace.[14]

While these petticoats could incorporate the necessary train it was sometimes more appropriate to have a separate layer of flounces that would button directly to the underside of the skirt train to keep it off the ground. This would also negate the need for a petticoat, further reducing perceived 'bulk'. Sometimes called 'dust ruffles', they were properly know as a 'balayeuse', a term that comes from the French and appropriately means 'female street-sweeper'. It also served a second purpose of supporting the train and giving it shape rather than it dragging behind in a crumpled manner, and since it was removable, it was easy to clean.

However, trained skirts were far from practical outdoors and 'dress holders' were often used to carry the train. Newspapers carried features on methods of carrying, the *Monmouthshire Merlin* suggested, 'over their arm like a riding habit, others sport a silver dress holder, but the most practical have a loop of ribbon sewn to the back of their skirt, and through this they pass a hand when walking.'[15] The latter was probably the most secure and easiest method; the 'dress holders' attached to the waist

The Natural Form era gown was figure hugging, the skirt drawn into the legs, often with a heavy train behind, c1876.

and clipped to the bottom of the skirt were somewhat unreliable, as one lady wrote in the *Leicester Chronicle* declaring, 'most are a delusion and a snare, coming undone and dropping the tail they pretend to grasp just as the unlucky wearer may be crossing a muddy street or when her hands are filled with parcels and an umbrella.'[16]

A more useful innovation that started to appear in the mid-1870s was the suspender belt. Previously stockings had been held up by simple garters fastened tightly either just above or just below the knee, which could be both uncomfortable and liable to slide down. The new suspender belt was fastened round the waist and had one long strap reaching down the outside of each leg, to just above the knee. The bottom of this split into two, each piece having a clip on the end to attach to the stocking. An advert appearing in numerous newspapers in 1876 appealed 'To Ladies – If you want comfort don't wear garters. If you want your children's legs tidy don't let them wear garters. If you want to avoid doctors' bills, don't wear garters, but order the New patent Stocking Suspender.'[17]

Stockings at this time were usually coloured, with striped and patterned stockings becoming popular towards the end of the decade. Cotton stocking would be worn for summer, merino for winter, silk was available but was generally kept for best as they were not so sturdy.

Three years later we find adverts for the intriguing 'Patent American Brace', not for holding up your stockings, but a combined back brace and skirt supporter. The benefits of this were extolled in its advertisements:

It expands the chest and gives free respiration to the lungs. It will keep the shoulders straight. Relieves back, hip, abdominal organs, by suspending the entire weight of the skirts from the shoulders. It entirely relieves the dragging down, weary feeling, and imparts new life to the wearer. It is worn without any inconvenience whatever, and is a positive comfort to the wearer.[18]

Accessories

The early 1870s were years of profusely decorated dresses and hairstyles became increasingly ornate. As the bulk of the skirt was now pushed backwards, so the hair similarly moved to the back of the head.

False hair was used to augment the huge styles of the 1870s. Heavy black jewellery was fashionable and not just for mourning, c.1875.

The bodice is trimmed 'en carré', simulating a low square neckline. The long chain may well have a watch on the end, tucked into a small pocket, note the false hair, c.1874.

Hair was bulky and piled high, chignons increased in size and moved upwards and could be augmented with plaits and knots, while ringlets could be seen cascading down the back. The bulk of these complex hairdos were made up of false hairpieces, the production and sale of which became big business.

France was the epicentre of the industry, in 1875 'the number of chignons exported from France to England was 16,820, with sufficient hair to make another 11,000'.[19] Much of the hair used came from the Continent, France and Italy being the the most popular, although the most expensive was red and golden hair coming mainly from Scotland. Rumours that hair was supplied by hospitals and cut from corpses was untrue for the simple reason that hair had to be 'live' to create the hairpieces, otherwise it was too brittle to work with. Cutters visited villages, country fairs and markets collecting hair, donors were not only paid in cash, but in goods such as shawls and dress materials. These cutters were employed by wholesale dealers to collect the hair, paying them a commission on what they collected.

Note how the slope of the low set sleeves, the cut of the bodice and bell shaped skirt emphasize the small waist, *Le Bon Ton* 1836.

The large gigot sleeves are now nothing more than a few ruffles, the hair smooth, centre parted and looped over the ears, *Le Follet*, June 1837.

Evening dresses and bonnets with flowers tucked inside the wide brims. *The World of Fashion & Monthly Magazine of the Courts of London & Paris*, March 1840.

The bodice is starting to lengthen, hair is worn in ringlets over the ears. *Townsend's Monthly Selection of Parisian Costumes*, June 1844.

Note the long bodice with a V neckline filled with a chemisette and the narrower, funnel like bonnet, *The World of Fashion & Monthly Magazine of the Courts of London & Paris*, May 1850.

Flounces were applied to the skirts to increase width, their decoration was *'a disposition'* to give the illusion of width, *Le Magasin des Familles*, September 1852.

The full crinoline with the pagoda sleeve was at its widest at this time. Note the close fitting bonnet lined under the brim with a white frill, *Les Modes Parisiennes*, c1857.

An ankle length walking skirt pulled up to reveal a coloured petticoat, the loose fitting jacket was starting to replace the cloak. *Englishwoman's Domestic Magazine, November 1863.*

The bodice and Zouave jacket show the now preferred bishop sleeve, the use of vivid aniline dye is becoming popular, *Englishwoman's Domestic Magazine*, January 1864.

Although the skirts are still voluminous the emphasis is starting to move to the back, *Englishwoman's Domestic Magazine*, April 1864.

With the crinoline gone, all emphasis was on the abundant decoration applied to skirt and bodice, c1873.

The voluminous hairstyles now in fashion pushed head-wear up and to the back of the head. *Journal des Demoiselles*, April 1876

With the bulk of the skirt now sitting at the back the figure is more slimline, *Englishwoman's Domestic Magazine*, 1877.

The skirt became very narrow with internal tapes pulling it in towards the legs, c1878.

The bustle now pushes the skirt straight out at the back, the front and sides are relatively straight. *The Young Ladies Journal*, November 1888.

A selection of outdoor garments, designed to compliment the bustle. *The Young Ladies Journal*, November 1888.

The distinct 1890s look is emerging as sleeves start to enlarge at the shoulder, *Weldon's Ladies' Journal*, May 1891.

The bustle has gone, skirts have a more slimline and plainer look. *Weldon's Ladies' Journal*, June 1892.

The sleeves would increase in size, reaching maximum proportions around mid decade before deflating. *Weldon's Ladies' Journal*, June 1893.

Short capes became popular as they were easy to wear over the inflated sleeves, *Weldon's Ladies' Journal*, October 1893.

James Greenwood wrote an atmospheric account of his visit to a human hair market In his book *In Strange Company, Being the Experiences of a Roving Correspondent* (1874):

> It was recently my privilege to inspect, and for just as long as I chose, linger over the enormous stock of the most extensive dealer in human hair in Europe. The firm in question has several warehouses, but this was the London warehouse, with cranes for lowering and hauling up heavy bales. I, however, was not fortunate in the selection of a time for my visit. The stock was running low, and a trifling consignment of seventeen hundredweight or so was at that moment lying at the docks till a waggon could be sent to fetch it away. But what remained of the impoverished stock was enough to inspire me with wonder and awe. On a sort of bench, four or five feet in width, and extending the whole length of the warehouse front, what looked like horse tails were heaped in scores and hundreds ; in the rear of this was another bench, similarly laden ; all round about were racks thickly festooned ; under the great bench were bales, some of them large almost as trusses of hay; and there was the warehouseman, with his sturdy bare arms, hauling out big handfuls of the tightly-packed tails, and roughly sorting them.[20]

Greenwood goes on to describe what he saw once the bales of hair were opened: 'Splendid specimens, every one of the tails. Eighteen or twenty inch lengths, soft and silky in texture, and many of rare shades of colour-chestnut, auburn, flaxen, golden.' The hair at this warehouse was European, although Greenwood explains that an attempt had been made to start trading with Japan but the hair was 'found to be too much like horsehair for the delicate purposes to which human hair is applied.'[21] Of all they colours they could seek the most sought after variety was the long silvery white hair from the elderly, simply because it could be dyed any colour.

The fashion for the abundant use of false hair pieces was relatively short lived, although the use of hair pieces never quite went away. As the slimmer, more vertical look took hold, so the hair subsided in response, relaxing into a simple, small, smooth chignon worn close to the head and often with a short curled or frizzed fringe by the end of the decade. The fringe was popularised by Alexandra, Princess of Wales, and those women who did not want to cut, or could not curl or frizz, their own hair used a small hairpiece called a 'frisette'. The year 1872 saw the appearance of deep waves, created by heavy, heated tongs, a look that would be revived and even more more pronounced in the 1930s when it was known as the 'Marcel Wave'. The vogue for the youngest ladies though was for them to wear a coil of hair down their back.

The mountain of hair in the early 1870s forced hats and bonnets upwards and forward, practically onto the forehead. Both items of headwear were now smaller to allow for the elaborate hairstyles and it was often difficult to differentiate between the two. Often they were only identifiable by the way they fastened: bonnets were tied under the chin, hats under the chignon, but by the mid-1870s these ribbons were often absent. Both were decorated with veils, lappets and ribbons dangling down the back, but they gradually became festooned with all manner of trimmings from bows and artificial flowers to feathers and whole stuffed birds. Styles of available hats and bonnets became numerous; among them were: the bergère, sailor hat (popularised by the Prince of Wales), the Tyrolese (small flat topped hat with tapering crown and narrow brim turned up on one side and sporting a feather cockade), the toque (usually of felt with a high crown and brim, trimmed with whole or part of a bird), a piffararo (chimney pot shaped with an aigrette in front), capote (hat with a soft crown often made of the same fabric as the dress). The latter years of the 1870s saw the Gainsborough bonnet become popular. This was a fitted velvet bonnet made of velvet or plush with a high curved brim and wide crown, often trimmed with a feather that would be worn at a rakish angle. As all these styles became popular in the 1870s the bonnet was seen as increasingly old fashioned and its popularity faded until, by the 1880s, it was worn predominantly for Sunday best and then only by older women.

Morning caps were also declining in popularity but at the start of the decade the Charlotte Corday, a full-crowned muslin cap named after a popular figure of the French Revolution, and the fanchon (like a handkerchief that tied under the chin, made from tulle, crêpe or silk and trimmed with bows, loops, ribbons, falls of lace or flowers and occasionally lappets) were popular. Like the fanchon, many morning caps were now bonnet-like, loosely tied under the chin by long lace

Hats were now more popular than bonnets and worn high on the head. Note the heavy velvet decoration on the bodice and large pendant, worn here by Ada Cavendish, actress c1872.

The hat is forced forward due to the bulk of the hair, note also the fashionably heavy dark chain and cross, c1873.

or muslin ties. By 1880 these too were being worn mainly by elderly women.

Towards the end of the 1860s the previously preferred shawl was becoming outmoded as the skirt changed shape. A very large shawl would sit beautifully on a dome shaped skirt, displayed in its full glory at the back, but did not sit well on a skirt that was bustled. Some enterprising ladies remodelled their shawls into mantles with a deft bit of needlework and the addition of a lining and trimmings. The mantle was popular, a kind of front-fastening, semi-fitted cape. Loose at the front but drawn in at the back at waist level (either internally or externally) and with pleats or a vent at the back to allow it to sit comfortably over the bustle. Often it would have long points at the front and one behind with the side pieces forming long, very loose sleeves. It could be fur lined in winter and trimmings were elaborate, with fringing being very common. Short mantles were also worn, often with a band of trimming down centre-back and heavily decorated.

Waist-length jackets became popular early on, these were double breasted and often with a turned-down collar and reveres. Sleeves were either long with cuffs, or pagoda shaped, some had obvious pockets on the front and early on they were highly trimmed with fringing, passementerie, lace or pleating. Capes and short shawls also had their place. Towards mid-decade trimmings became less, but there was a fad for very large buttons. As the bustle diminished and the Natural Form came in, so the jacket slimmed down. By the end of the decade it was well fitted and could be three quarter-length, trimmings were usually minimal. The loss of the bustle allowed the adoption of previously masculine outer garments such as the Chesterfield and caped Ulster.

Fabrics and colours of the 1870s

Listed below are some of the most common fabrics and popular colours as recorded in fashion magazines, pattern books and adverts of the 1870s.

Albert crêpe, alpaca, armure, armurette, ballernos, barathea, barège, batiste, bourrette, brocade, broche silk, bure, cambric, camlet, carmeline, cashmere, China crêpe, corduroy, Crêpe de chine, crêpeline, cretonne, damask, drap de France, duchesse satin, faille, flannel, foulard (plain, spotted), frou frou, galatea (plain, striped), gauze, Holland, Genoa velvet, gingham, glacé, grenadine, gros de Rome, gros grain, Imperial velvet, jacconete, Japanese pongee, Japanese silk (plain, striped, checked, corded, patterned), knickerbocker, limousine, linen, linsey, Madras, mariposa, matelassé, melton, merino, Mikado, mohair, muslin, natté, neigeuse, Pekin, Pekin brocades, percale, plush, poil de chevre, pompadour silk, poplin, poult de soie, sateen (plain or patterned), satin, satin jean, serge, serge royale, Shantung pongee, Sicilienne, silk, silk velvet sultane, surah, taffeta, tamative, tarlatan, thibet, tripoline, tulle, tussore, velvet, velveteen, vicuna, vigogne.

Almond, amethyst, biscuit, black, blue, blue-green, blue grey, brick red, bronze, brown, canary yellow, cardinal red, cerise, chestnut, claret, coral, cream, dark blue, dark green, dark grenat, dark indigo, dove grey, eau de nil, écru, electric blue, emerald, faded rose, fawn, garnet, gold, green, green bronze, grenat, grey, Havannah brown, indigo, ink blue, light brown, light canary, light green, linden green, maize, mandarin, maroon, mastic, mauve, Mexican blue, mignonette (greenish grey), moonbeam (grey-green), moss green, myrtle green, old gold, olive, olive brown, olive green, orange, pale blue, pale nenuphar green, peacock blue, pink, plaids, plum, red, ruby, Russian leather, sage green, scarlet, sea green, salmon pink, silver grey, sulphur, sultan red, terracotta, turquoise, turtle-dove, violet, white, wood.

Four beautifully tailored outfits, the sleeves are starting to expand at the shoulder, c.1889.

Chapter 5

1880s

The final years of Victoria's reign, the Late Victorian or Aesthetic Era (1885–1901), were a period of increasing change in the attitude and outlook of more and more women. They were starting to question their perceived place in society; why they couldn't vote, work after marriage, study; why was their role simply to bear children and look after husband home and family? There was also a growing interest in leading a healthier lifestyle, from diet, to exercise and dress. This led to the likes of Dr Jeagers Sanitary Wool System and the Rational Dress Movement who pushed for, among other things, more appropriate clothing for cycling. For everyday dress the emphasis moved to the back of the skirt, with the bustle becoming the defining feature of the decade, the years it was in fashion were also known as the Second Bustle Era.

The 1880s Look

At the turn of the new decade the bustle for daywear was gone, the whole costume was now slim and 'sheath like'. Hems rose to brush the top of the foot and trains were generally reserved for evening wear, and without the weight of the fabric pulling the skirts back they became almost tubular, the look was more severe than the ruffled and flounced look of the 1870s. Skirts could have broad bands of pleating to the knee or could even be pleated to the waist, the lining being tight to ensure the pleats were preserved. Ruching, bows and ribbon trimmings were also popular and, along with drapes worn over the skirt, produced a myriad of looks. These could be asymmetrical, turned back from the front like revers, or open to the side. Early 1880 saw a brief return to popularity for the polonaise; long, slim-fitting and fastened either at the front or behind, it now sported a line of gathers centre-front, about ten inches long, pulling the lower front up. Occasionally it can be seen gathered at one side, giving a slanted look. Outfits would be made in contrasting colours and textures, meaning multiple fabrics could be seen in one look, there was a preference for soft heavy fabrics such as velvet and plush (a long-piled cotton velvet) and dark rich colours.

By 1882 the elaborate drapes sometimes worn over the skirt created residual puffs at the hips, the start of the resurgence of the bustle. In the previous decade the bustled look had been produced mainly by the cut of the skirt, it now took on an identity of its own, becoming a garment itself. This new bustle was more pronounced, projecting sharply outwards, and since skirts now lacked a train, the drapery of the bustle fell sharply downwards at an angle towards the hem of the now ground-length skirt. The acute

A lovely tweed outfit with a pointed cuirass bodice, the chain would have a watch on the end tucked into a small pocket, c1880.

angle of the new bustle could only really be appreciated when viewed from the side, as the the front and back remained quite narrow compared the the earlier bustle fashion. This drapery took on various styles from simple to asymmetrical, to swathes of fabric caught up on one side and often with an 'apron' of draped fabric worn across the front. As the bustle grew, the highly trimmed look of the early 1880s fell out of favour as the preferred look for everyday wear became much plainer and the 'tailor-made' outfit came to the fore, more or less unique in the fact that its origin was English rather than French.

During the 1880s, middle-class women were not only entering the workplace in greater numbers than before, they were also starting to take on a more active and healthier lifestyle. The early years of the decade saw 'tailor-made' outfits that could adapt to a wider range of activities become popular, particularly for walking. They were cut like the fitted bodice but had revers and collars, they were made from sturdier fabrics like wool, tweed and serge – fabrics often used for men's suits – and were so

S P E N C E ' S   D R E S S E S.

WHOLESALE CITY PRICES.   PATTERNS POST-FREE.

1884. | LATEST NOVELTIES IN DRESS. | 1884.

With the multiplicity of **New Materials** for the present Season it is impossible for Ladies residing in the Country to obtain so good a selection as they can in **London**. J. S. and Co. therefore recommend Ladies to write for their **New Collection of Patterns**, sent **post-free**, of which they have over 10,000 to select from, representing all the **New Cloths** made for the present Season. J. S. and Co. buy direct from the **Manufacturers**, and in many cases have **Novelties** made specially and solely for themselves; they are enabled to mark their goods at such prices for **Cash** as will always command a ready sale. On no account is any extra **Profit** calculated for **Novelties**, sole reliance being placed upon the extensive and ready sale which has always been a great success with them.

N.B.—PATTERNS POST-FREE.

Ladies are requested to send a Post-Card stating what class of Goods are required, and about what price desired, and a first-class Selection will be sent by return of post, free.

SPENCE'S
WASHING   MATERIALS.

THE LARGEST AND BEST COLLECTION IN LONDON.
PATTERNS POST-FREE TO ALL PARTS OF THE GLOBE.   1884.

It is impossible to give Ladies even a faint idea of the number and diversity of Patterns and Fabrics. Suffice it to say we have collected from the FRENCH, ENGLISH, SCOTCH, and IRISH MANUFACTURERS over 1000 different and distinct patterns, representing every cloth made for the Season. Many of these Patterns are made specially and solely for us.

The Novelties consist of a large variety of all the leading productions in Zephyr, French and English Prin'ed Sateens, and other new features in Cotton Dress Materials for 1884, manufactured expressly for JAMES SPENCE and CO.
Patterns Post-free.

SPENCE'S DRESS NOVELTIES, 1884.

In this Department it is impossible to detail all our varied and general Stock, but we submit some of the leading Novelties for the coming Season with our standard Cloths that we have always in stock—Mourning and other Black Goods. As we are having novelties in both British and Foreign Dress Materials delivered from the manufacturers almost daily, Ladies would do well to write for our patterns at any time of the year when requiring New Dresses. We would call special attention to the splendid range of Colourings of all our Cloths. We always order between thirty and forty colours to be dyed in every new Cloth we offer to our patrons, thus giving an immense variety of shades to choose from.

SPENCE'S NEW ILLUSTRATED PRICE-LIST,

Just published, contains the prices current in the different departments for this season. Splendid Illustrations of the latest Costumes, Mantles, Ulsters, Laces, Gloves, Jerseys, Corsets, Haberdashery, Cabinets, Umbrellas, &c. Over Eighty Illustrations. Every lady should write for a copy, which will be sent free.

SPENCE'S ACCORDION COSTUME.
Made by the patent Kilting Machine.
Price £2 5s. 9d. (as Illustration).

No. 1, Skirt made of SPENCE'S NUN'S CLOTH,
with long length for Bodice, complete £2 5 9
No. 2, Skirt made of FINEST CASHMERE,
with long length for Bodice, complete 2 7 6
No. 3, Skirt made of RICH SURAH SILK,
with long length for Bodice, complete 3 9 6
No. 4, Skirt made of RICH DUCHESSE SATIN,
with long length for Bodice, complete 3 13 6

N.B.—10s. 6d. extra charged for making and lining Bodice complete. In ordering, kindly state size of waist and length of skirt in front. Patterns (40 shades) of the Materials of which the above Costume is made sent free.

SPENCE'S PROMENADE COSTUME.
Price £2 5s. 9d. (as Illustration).
Handsomely trimmed with New Saxony Lace & Ribbon.

No. 1, Skirt made of SPENCE'S NUN'S CLOTH,
with long length for Bodice, complete £2 5 9
No. 2, Skirt made of FINEST CASHMERE,
with long length for Bodice, complete 2 7 6
No. 3, Skirt made of RICH SURAH SILK,
with long length for Bodice, complete 3 9 6
No. 4, Skirt made of RICH DUCHESSE SATIN,
with long length for Bodice, complete 3 13 6

N.B.—10s. 6d. extra charged for making and lining Bodice complete. In ordering, kindly state size of waist and length of skirt in front. Patterns (40 shades) of the Materials of which the above Costume is made sent free.

JAMES SPENCE and CO., St. Paul's-churchyard, London.

Illustrated London News, May 1884.

named because they were made by a gentleman's tailor rather than a lady's dressmaker. They were smart and unfussy, but still with the fashionable bustle. By the end of the decade the bustle was gone and 'tailor-made' carried on with the new-look gored skirt. Still made from thicker fabrics, the skirt was untrimmed and worn with a high-necked blouse and fitted jacket. Not all magazines were in favour of this new look, *The Queen* in 1883 declared 'All dresses – be they of habit cloth, tweed, serge or any woollen material – are however made in simple and in many cases almost severe style; perfect fit and excellence of workmanship alone being relied on to produce the – we must say it – mannish effect, which is unhappily the prevailing taste.'

Masculine touches could be seen in the form of a waistcoat, tie and straw boater. The general simplicity of look, and the fact they were made from hard wearing fabrics, meant they were easy to care for. To complement such outfits, a lady could also purchase specially designed walking boots 'of black or bronze kid, made with from seventeen to twenty-four very small buttons for dressy toilets; of patent leather, with cloth gaiters buttoned half-way up the leg, for more negligée dress and for travelling.'[1]

The bodice shortened to above the hips to accommodate the bustle but had a pointed front, with the fashionable high-fitted mandarin, or officer collar, tight sleeves and small buttons all the way up the front. Bodices could be double breasted coming only to the waist, two tails behind sat on the bustle and with small reveres at the neck folded back to show a cravat-like tie with a pin in the middle. The cravat was very quickly replaced by a closed collar with a brooch pinned at the neck. The plain, high-necked bodice had a look that could be quite severe, even business-like, often the only softening of this look was a glimpse of white frill at the cuff and neck.

As the 1880s progressed, some tight-fitting bodices were designed with central panels and revers, imitating a jacket and waistcoat, often in different colours or fabrics. They could be pointed front and back at the bottom or simply straight. The front panel, or plastron, could be pleated vertically or gathered top and bottom, creating a puffed effect down the centre front of the bodice. The plastron was either applied onto the front or revealed by the bodice opening. Sleeves started long and tight, sometimes with a cuff and white frill, and were set high on the shoulder. Around about 1882 they developed a slight fullness at the shoulder and were either down to the wrist or three quarter-length, and by the end of the decade some had increased in fullness all the way down, resembling a narrower version of the old 'bishop sleeve'. Velvet collars and cuffs became popular c.1887 and the look of a relatively simple bodice contrasting with a complicated-looking skirt stayed in fashion for the rest of the decade

In the mid-1880s a craze for tricycling for men – and to a lesser degree, women – took hold. In her book *The Science of Dress in Theory & Practice*, Miss Ada S. Ballin encouraged women to take up tricycling extolling its virtues as affording:

both healthy and delightful exercise for women, for whom it is especially suited by the absence of jolting, and the manner in which the body is supported, which **two** characteristics render it more healthful for our sex than horse-riding.[2]

She further encouraged the healthy hobby saying that 'the ladies of the Royal Family have set a good example to the women of England in this matter', explaining that Princess Mary, Duchess of Teck, and Princess Louise already ride tricycles, and that Queen Victoria herself presented her granddaughters, the princesses of Hesse, with them.

As to the appropriate clothing to wear for the pursuit, Miss Ballin points out that several dresses adapted for tricycle wear were displayed at the International Health Exhibition at Kensington, 1884, and described them as, 'neat dark cloth costumes, ulsters or jackets, with small felt or cloth hats to match … or dresses of those brownish materials which do not show the dust of the road.[3] One of the outfits was also intended for mountaineering purposes:

Fig. 23.

A tricycling outfit consisting of a Norfolk style bodice and a skirt with full length kilting to allow pedalling, 1885.

made of dark blue cloth with gaiters, knickerbockers, a skirt reaching to the knees and a very pretty short coat like a gentleman's shooting jacket, with a hat to match…. This sort of dress saves the wearer from the friction and weight of long skirts, which form an impediment, and are the means of wasting a considerable amount of energy, whether in walking or propelling a machine.[4]

Mr T.W. Goodman, personal tailor to Miss Ballin, designed ladies' costumes specifically for tricycling. One of his dress designs had 'a smart jacket body, the skirt being plain with a number of pleats inserted as deep kilting at the front, partially concealed by a pointed apron. The pleats provide accommodation for the knee when it rises in working the machine.'[5] Although still bustled at the back and, on the surface, giving a slim-fitting, flat-fronted fashionable outline, this outfit would provide far more freedom of movement. All Mr Goodman's tricycling outfits were lined in flannel and it was recommended that they be worn with woollen combinations next to the skin with 'a flannel body fitting closely to the figure to take the place of stays, and buttoned on to this a pair of knickerbockers or trousers of cloth to match the dress.'[6] These, of course, would not be seen, but Miss Ballin commented that such clothing 'gives a sense of lightness and freedom which can never be enjoyed by one dressed in the ordinary way.'[7]

Another sporting activity that had gradually increased in popularity over the previous two decades was swimming, and the late 1880s saw swimming clubs for girls starting up as competitions became popular. The *Girls Own Paper* describes the latest swimwear fashion as having two designs 'the combination trousers and corsage worn with a belt and short tunic … and trousers made separately and the upper part in blouse shape with a band'.[8] The 'blouse' was actually a garment that fell to the thigh and a 'band' was a belt.

Fabrics used for swimwear were often sturdy and quite thick, such as serge and cretonne; at the start of the 1880s bathing dresses were generally high-necked, but became lower throughout the decade. Dresses were usually blue or red with a sailor collar and trimmed with white braid, though some blue outfits had red braid. Feet were protected by straw-soled shoes with embroidered linen uppers. The same magazine also mentions the fact that some ladies who were good swimmers 'adopted the striped woollen jersey of the fisherman, and wear it with full knickerbockers of blue serge'.[9]

Other sports, such as tennis, were still played wearing corsets, bodice and bustled skirts, although skirts did tend to be a little shorter:

For lawn tennis no special dress is required, but jerseys are very comfortable to play in, and on the whole the prettiest tennis dresses are those made in white flannel with loose sailor bodices.[10]

Initially any colour was acceptable, but by the time 19-year-old Maud Watson beat her sister Lilian to become the first Wimbledon Ladies' Singles Championship in 1884, pale or white garments were recommended because they were better at masking perspiration. The 1880s not only saw the creation of special lawn tennis pinafores with special pockets to hold the balls, but also the availability of ready-made tennis outfits. In 1887,

Dickins & Jones's Summer Catalogue included what were described as 'a very large assortment of new unshrinkable lawn tennis flannels. Also the tennis or boating jacket in fancy striped flannel and plain cream and colours, well shrunk and tailor-made.'[11]

Shooting suits were also available, consisting of a Norfolk jacket with a just below knee-length box-pleated skirt worn over knickerbockers and long gaiters. Under the gaiters, particularly later in the decade, there were high-buttoned boots or lace-up shoes worn over black stockings.

Buttericks Patterns & Weldon's *Ladies' Journal*

For those ladies who maybe couldn't afford to purchase off the peg, or have made for them, the market for the latest fashions in dressmaking patterns was booming. Buttericks, which started in the US in 1863, set up its first shop in London ten years later. Within a few years its premises expanded from one to three big houses on Regent Street. By the 1880s they employed thirty to forty staff at their London site, and their factory at Chalk Farm produced between forty to sixty new designs a month.

Some bodices were designed with central panels and revers, imitating a jacket and waistcoat. Hairstyles were now a simple chignon at the back, c.1883.

This young lady is proudly showing off her chatelaine.

Priced from 3d to 2/- there was something for everyone, and unlike many of the free patterns issued with magazines, which had multiple designs on one sheet (the required pieces would have to be carefully copied out if you wanted to make more than one garment), these were simpler and easier to use. These patterns were sold not only at their London site, but via some 200–400 agents, usually drapers' shops, throughout the country. Buttericks advertised their designs through coloured fashion plates that they sent to their agents as well as tailors and dressmakers. The company also had their own printing department and produced a number of magazines in 1887, including *The Delineator*, *The Ladies' Monthly Review*, *The Quarterly Report of Metropolitan Fashions* and *The Tailors' Review*.

Foundation Garments

The sheath-like look of the late 1870s was not to last very long. The early 1880s saw the reappearance of a small bustle pad, but very soon the bustle returned with a vengeance and from c.1882 it continued to grow in size. The new bustle was narrower, placed several inches lower than previously and centred at the back rather than spreading over the hips. The bustle reached its maximum size 1887–1888, diminishing in size quite quickly after that.

The crinolette from the 1870s resurfaced early on and evolved into the bustle cage, it was also called 'dress improver' or 'tournure', because the word bustle was now considered vulgar. Probably the most recognisable 'tournure' is what became known as the 'lobster tail', with its horizontal semi-circular boning gradually increasing in size from waist to lower calf. It sat behind the hips, projecting outwards. It would then smoothed around the sides and front of the body by flat, shaped pieces of fabric, keeping the skirt-front smooth but supporting it at the back. No longer made simply in white or natural colours, the bustles of the 1880s could be striped, coloured or highly patterned. Although it could be rather cumbersome the bustle was more comfortable than the very tight skirts of some of the earlier fashions. There are stories of bustles being so big that you could balance a tea tray on them; however, it must be remembered that, as with the corset and crinoline cage, extremes of size were the exception rather than the rule and most bustles were of a size that was practical for the wearer in their everyday life.

The bodice has shortened to accommodate the re-emerging bustle, coming to a point at the front and with tight sleeves and a high mandarin collar, c.1883.

A beautifully fitted and decorated short cuirass bodice, you can just see the bustle protruding at the back, c1884.

There were numerous options for the discerning and fashion-conscious lady when it came to purchasing a bustle, and they came in all shapes and sizes. There was the 'Keelapso' bustle, described in its advertising as:

light (weighing under 4ozs), cool, well fitting, and correct in shape; it is firm enough to hold the heaviest of garments without crushing. It collapses entirely when the wearer sits down, and, when rising, instantly resumes its proper shape, and is so easy and comfortable that she forgets she is wearing a bustle.[12]

The 'Langtry' bustle was a similar idea, and named after one of the most famous actresses of the day, Lily Langtry. There was also the 'Health' bustle made out of a wire mesh which allowed it to breathe and circulate the air, and Stapley and Smith's ingenious 'New Phantom' bustle, made with metal wire hoops on a pivot that folded themselves away when the wearer sat down and fell back into place when she stood up. Some were simply colourful cushions padded with horsehair, down, or even straw to achieve the required shape. There was even a novelty bustle produced to commemorate Queen Victoria's Golden Jubilee in 1887 that was fitted with a musical box that would play God Save The Queen whenever the wearer sat down. By 1888 the bustle was starting to collapse and by the end of 1890 it was a thing of the past, and simple padding took its place rounding out the hips.

It wasn't just bustles that became more decorative, corsets did too; they could now be purchased in bold colours like reds and yellows along with the usual neutral colours. More decoration was seen in the form of lace and decorative embroidery on the boning channels, which also served to keep the bones in place. They were heavily boned, with the spoon busk still being popular. The manufacture of ready-to-wear corsets had improved; not only were they now available in different bust and hip measurements, but for different body types from 'full' to 'graceful'. Just as in previous decades there were also means of improving the figure, Worth's Patent Palpitating Bust Improvers were advertised for 'ladies both slim and stout…. To slim figures they give a perfectly natural fullness, while for stout ladies they afford great comfort and support. Are easily attached to any corset.'[13]

If you didn't want to pad your clothing there were lotions and creams to be had, such as Madame Marie Fontaine's Bosom Beautifier from America whose advertising cards boldly claimed that her product 'will in every instance where the directions are faithfully followed, enlarge and beautify the bosom, in both old and young ladies…. It not only increases the size and hardens the bosoms but gives to them the beautiful transparency so much admired.

In the spirit of promoting health, and mindful after unfortunate accidents had occurred due to fashion clothing, accessories or preparations, Fontaine reassured potential purchasers that her product was indeed safe and took pains to point out that 'It contains nothing injurious to the skin, on the contrary, it is a certain remedy for blotches, moth, discolouration, pimples and other blemishes of the skin.[14]

It even boasted 'a delightful and elegant' perfume, and in the early days of celebrity association with, and even endorsement of, products every one of these advertising cards depicted an attractive young woman wearing the device, accompanied by a portrait of the aesthetic poet Oscar Wilde, a man well known at that time for his appreciation of the female form.

NOS. 1 AND 2.—SKIRTS FOR HOME OR WALKING DRESSES.

NO. 3.—HOME-DRESS.

NO. 4.—DRESSING-SLIPPER.

NO. 5.—DINNER-DRESS.

NO. 6.—CRAVAT-BOW.

NO. 7.—CRAVAT-BOW.

NO. 8.—DINNER-DRESS.

NOS. 9 AND 10.—WALKING DRESSES.

NO. 11.—HOME-DRESS.

The Young Ladies' Journal, March 1884.

Since clothing was still tight, the design of chemise and drawers continued to reduce bulk under the snug-fitting garments. The *Young Ladies Journal* describes a new style of drawers and petticoat 'so that all unnecessary fullness round the waist is done away with; the drawers have a wide band, with buttons on the lower edge; buttonholes to correspond are made in the narrow band of the petticoat, so that it may be buttoned to the drawers.'[15] Both the chemise and drawers could be made from wool for warmth, but also fine lawn, muslin and silk, trimmed with lace, embroidery and threaded with ribbons making them extremely feminine.

The increase in physical activities for women led to greater strain on certain areas of the corset, which in turn led to incidences of corset bones snapping and either piercing the skin or poking through the dress. From 1885 adverts began to appear for the likes of 'Browns Dermathistic Corset', for 'ladies who indulge in such healthful and exhilarating exercises as rowing, riding, driving, lawn tennis &c'.[16] The corset was unusual in that all boning channels were faced in leather, 'being a sure prevention against bones, busks or side steels breaking, while it renders the corset most delightfully pliable to the figure during the most active or violent exertions, thus making it for general wear, comfort and durability the most useful corset ever invented.'[17] The adverting also quoted reviews from fashion journals, such as this glowing review from *Myra's Journal of Dress and Fashion*: 'an ingenious method of insuring durability. The leather adds in no way to the bulk, while it gives a decided added support to the figure, besides preventing wear. They are very comfortable.'[18]

Black stockings were becoming the usual daywear wear for most women and while silk stockings were still an expensive luxury, the 1880s saw the availability of the more affordable alternative of cotton stockings that had been chemically treated to resemble silk. One of the largest manufacturers of these stockings was I & R Morley of Nottingham. This family business had made their name through producing good quality stockings and received Royal patronage. In the 1880s Morleys had ten factories and smart London warehouses, their catalogues offered thousands of items and at the company's peak in 1886, it had 10,000 employees on its payroll.

Accessories

Following the very heavy, some may say vulgar, jewellery that was fashionable in the 1870s, the 1880s were a complete contrast as fewer, more delicate items of jewellery became the fashion. Silver was still popular for bracelets, necklaces and brooches. Cut gems were somewhat out of favour in the early 1880s with chased metal far more in vogue. Popular designs typical of this period involved flowers, insects, birds and mottos or inscriptions, jet also remained popular. The gemstones that were in vogue were almost colourless moonstones and strings of pearls that would both be subtly enhanced by the new electric lighting being fitted in homes, theatres and restaurants.

Queen Victoria had been made Empress of India back in 1877 and with that came a renewed interest in Indian made and Indian style jewellery, furnishings, rugs and carpets. In 1886 the Industrial Arts of India Exhibition was held in London sparking a vogue for handmade Indian jewellery. However, by the late 1880s so little jewellery was being worn during the daytime that there was a temporary crisis in the trade and the Birmingham Jewellers Association called on Alexandra, princess of Wales, to help. The princess was known to have such an influence on fashion that by simply being seen at public occasions, being photographed and depicted in illustrations in popular magazines wearing more jewellery, the fashionable lady of the time would follow suit.

The neater hairdos that became popular with the sheath-like dress carried on into the 1880s. The high mandarin collars that accompanied the tight fitting tailored bodices ensured that the long cascading curls and hairpieces were finally gone for good and were replaced by tight chignons. These in turn crept onto the top of the head, often just leaving a curled fringe of real or fake hair showing from under the hat or bonnet. Well known actress and society beauty Lily Langtry not only lent her name to a brand of 'tournure' but also to a hairstyle, the 1883 'Lily Langtry Wave' was a curled coiffure with a crimped fringe and low chignon worn on the back of the neck.

The wearing of indoor caps was now restricted to breakfast time, and disappeared completely during the decade. Both hats and bonnets were now worn firmly on top of the head, the former were again worn with a wide ribbon tied under the chin. Hats quickly grew in height, becoming quite tall and tapering to the crown. One popular number being the 'postilion', with a tall crown and narrow brim turned up at the sides or back, another was the 'gable' bonnet, so called because the front came to a high point. More unusual styles seen mid- to late decade include the tam o'shanter and sailor hats with large bows, for sporting purposes a jockey-style cap could be seen. The height of the hats provided plenty of space for decoration which could be quite elaborate with ribbons, flowers lace, feathers, and even small stuffed mammals or whole birds. The use of tropical birds, or parts of, became prolific during this time. Not used just by milliners to adorn hats, but also to create accessories and decorate dresses.

A beautiful masculine military style bodice softened by the addition of lace cuffs, c1886.

The *Young Ladies Journal* for January 1884 reported that 'exotic birds are much sought after as ever; they are placed in little nests of tulle or gauze upon the front of a low bodice, or by way of a bouquet on a short sleeve. Handsome butterflies are the rivals of such tiny birds.'[19] A single consignment of birds from South America might contain 40,000 hummingbirds. Not everyone condoned the practice of adorning their person with dead birds however, and in 1889 a group of ladies in Manchester formed the 'Fur, Fin & Feather Folk' to fight the deadly trade. The late 1880s saw both hats and bonnets becoming smaller again, but the illusion of height was kept by tall pointed feathers, pairs of bird's wings rising vertically from the front of the crown, or even whole birds with wings folded back and tails pointing upwards.

Complimenting the headwear, prior to the re-emergence of the bustle, long coats with pleats at the back seam called Pelisses were popular, but the new bustle fashion ensured that the previously slim outdoor garments had to be side-lined in favour of things that would sit smartly with the bustle. Shorter cloaks reappeared, this time they often had a turned-up collar and long ribbon ties at the throat. Mantles or dolmans became popular again, they were now high-collared, long down the front and shorter behind so they could sit on top of the bustle, emphasising it further. The sleeves were cut with the body of the garment making them less restricting than a jacket or coat, and they were often heavily trimmed with the likes of fringe, feathers and passementerie, and accessorised with a fur muff.

Hand-knitting was also a popular pastime; in the 1840s and 1850s, Jane Gaugain wrote a number of knitting pattern books, notably the *Lady's Assistant in Knitting, Netting*

The bustled skirt made way for the simpler gored skirt, worn here with a very fashionable straw boater, c.1888.

and Crochet', which proved to be extremely popular and ran to twenty-two editions. The Crimean War (1853–1854) also saw ladies magazines producing patterns for Balaclava helmets, scarves and other 'comforts'. However, until the end of the 1870s knitted garments for ladies were generally confined to petticoats, shawls, bed jackets, wraps, purses and children's clothes. The 1880s saw a new resurgence in home knitting as Weldon's began producing a well illustrated monthly magazine entitled *Practical Needlework* and began issuing a sub-series of *Practical Knitter* that offered patterns for 'useful garments for Ladies, Gents and Children' at the competitive price of 2d an edition in 1886. However, it would not be until 1899 that the first dedicated knitting pattern book, the *Universal Knitting Book*, would be published by the knitting yarn manufacturer John Paton, Son & Co of Alloa, Scotland. Both Weldons and Patons enjoyed huge success with their printed knitting patterns which continued long into the twentieth century.

Dr Gustav Jaeger, his Sanitary Wool System and the Dawn of Aertex

Dr Gustav Jaeger of Stuttgart published his first book on the effect clothing had on health in Germany in 1878. The translated tracts of his lectures and booklets outlining his theories were soon translated and circulated across Europe:

> The skin is pierced by millions of pores, through which is consistently exhaled a watery vapour, whereby the body is relived of much matter that would be poisonous if suppressed or retained. The chief desideratum, therefore, in the body's covering is that the skins function of exhalation should suffer as little impediment as possible, and here two points must be chiefly considered:- The covering should be pervious throughout, to permit the exhalation to escape. The skins should be maintained at an equable warmth, as any chill diminishes activity, driving away the blood to the internal organs.

He goes on to explain:

> The vital function of exhalation performed by the pores of the skin has a very great influence on the health, so much so, indeed, that if this function be suspended by artificially closing the pores, even for a short time, death will ensue.[20]

Jaeger offered the opinion that fabrics made from plant fibres such as linen and cotton were detrimental to this 'exhalation' and should be avoided at all costs. He advocated instead that a person should only wear wool, from underwear to outerwear and right down to pocket, clothing and boot linings, all bedding and even upholstered furniture should also be made of wool. By doing this himself, he swore that he had cured himself of chronic ill health.

Jaeger's introduction to Britain came courtesy of Lewis Tomalin, manager of a grocery wholesale firm in London. He was so convinced by Dr Jaeger's claims that he secured the sole rights to use the Jaeger name in Britain, along with all systems and patents that went with it. He promptly burned all the non-woollen clothing and bedding he owned.

In early 1884 he started to manufacture 100 per cent woollen Jaeger clothing at premises he had obtained at 42 and 43 Fore Street in City of London. Jaeger produced both underwear and outer clothing for men, women and children to his own designs. Every necessary item of clothing was available under his Sanitary Woollen System, stockings (including 'digitated hosiery' – socks with toes), stocking suspenders, shawls and wraps, knee warmers, gloves, corsets, petticoats, night dresses, under vests for cold weather with a double thickness of wool over the chest for warmth, drawers, chemise, combinations, skirts and bodices. Jaeger was careful to advise that for his system to be successful it should be adopted in its entirety.

Underclothing was made from 'Stockinette Web', a knitted fabric, and the range of colours for all items was somewhat limited, mainly natural shades of browns and creams, black, indigo and for evening shawls, claret or biscuit was available. The recommended outfit for a woman included the Sanitary Woollen Corset, which promised to be flexible, elastic and durable, responding to every movement of the body and with steels that could be removed for cleaning:

> Such a corset over the woollen underclothing, and beneath a woollen dress, lined (if at all) with woollen lining, allows the skin to breathe, promoting a feeling of health, buoyancy, and a freedom from oppressive heat.[21]

The dress in question sported long, tight sleeves and a high, tight neck to prevent draughts. There was also the Jaeger Corset Bodice, made of finely woven unbleached wool. This garment laced at the back but also buttoned right down the front, it was more flexible than the corset as it was corded with twisted wool cords, rather than boned. It had shoulder straps and bust sections of knife-pleated wool; it was deemed particularly appropriate for maids because its support and flexibility aided them in their work.

Many dress reformists believed that putting the bulk of the weight of the skirts on the waist and hips was not healthy, adding shoulder straps to a corset moved the weight to the shoulders which they believed to be better for both the spine and internal organs.

In the autumn of 1884 Tomalin secured a place at the International Health Exhibition in London and won a gold medal for his stand. Doctors had already testified in the *British Medical Journal* that the clothing system relieved rheumatism and consequently these, along with famous patrons like Oscar Wilde and George Bernard Shaw, ensured a throng of enthusiastic customers visited Tomalin's stores. Its followers were known as 'Woollenites' or 'Woolleners' and the Jaeger brand carried on successfully for over a century.

Mr Lewis Haslam also believed in the health benefits of breathable fabrics and the fact they would help insulate the body against heat and cold by trapping air. Jaeger's love for wool directly on the skin was all well and good, but it ultimately became felted with washing, reducing its breathable qualities. In 1887 Haslam, along with Sir Benjamin Ward Richardson and Dr Richard Green, began to experiment with the trapping of air within the warp and weft of fabrics at a Bolton Mill. The result was the invention of a new breathable fabric they called 'Aertex'. So novel was the idea it took just one sales representative armed with samples travelling from Lands End to John 'O Groats to achieve nationwide sales. In 1888 the Cellular Clothing Company was set up to produce the Aertex material which was initially only sold as a fabric to clothing manufacturers to produce their own garments. Aertex soon expanded into their own men's clothing production at units in Nottingham, opened their own outlets in a prime location in Piccadilly and sold throughout the country. Aertex began catering for the women's market in 1891, predominantly producing vests, combinations and corsets.

The Rational Dress Movement

Throughout the Victorian period there was always a reform movement opposing the fashion trends of the times. The reformists came from various groups, including health advocates and feminists. The corset was a particular target for the reformists, especially the perceived evils of tight lacing. They vilified it for its alleged health concerns, including the damaging and rearranging of internal organs, circulatory problems and an adverse effect on fertility, claiming it was a foolish vanity that women would compromise their health for the sake of fashion. Those who were pro-corset on the other hand, claimed that it was not only required for stylish dress but also that it aided the correct upright and healthy posture. Over the decades the dress reformers found problems with many of the fashions that appeared, including concerns that women could not move freely, and therefore could not exercise, due to the layers of petticoat, skirt, crinoline, bustle and high heels. The vivid aniline dyes and profuse decoration were also frowned upon.

The Artistic Dress movement of the 1840s had never really fully gone away. The 1870s saw a rise in the popularity of what was now called Aesthetic Dress. The increase in popularity was enough for renowned fashion magazine *The Queen* to commission articles on the subject by journalist Eliza Mary Haweis author of *The Art of Dress* (1879). The Aesthetic movement dresses were high-waisted and flowing, in a push against aniline dyes, colours were natural and the fabrics were often patterned, Japonaise designs and those created by Liberty of London were particularly sought after. The silk and wool fabrics from Liberty proved so popular among the Aesthetic Dress movement that in 1884 they opened the Liberty & Co. Artistic and Historic Costume Studio, and in 1889 presented their Aesthetic gowns at the Paris *Exposition Universalle*.

One of Liberty's most popular fabrics was one they called 'Umritza', it was a form of cashmere popular not only because it was lightweight and soft, but also because it was durable. While Aesthetic gowns borrowed elements from both the classical and medieval eras, with an emphasis on the natural shape, they were distinctly Victorian in look. Considered somewhat daring as they were worn without corsets and bustles, but it should be noted that even the loosest looking gowns often concealed lightly boned bodices to give support. Like the Artistic movement, the Aesthetic movement had its well known supporters, among them Oscar and Constance Wilde, the former wearing a velvet jacket and knee breeches as his 'aesthetic lecturing costume' for a lecturing tour of America in 1882. Alice Comyns Carr, head costume designer for the actress Ellen Terry, was also among the high-profile supporters of the movement.

While the Aesthetic movement looked to a more romanticised appearance, there was another organisation that looked to promote a more practical approach to clothing for Victorian women. The Rational Dress Society was founded in London in 1881 with co-founder Lady

Florence Harbeton as its president. Lady Harberton was an advocate of the practicality of the divided skirt, particularly for cycling. Unlike the Bloomer costume of the early 1850s, which consisted of a mid-calf-length skirt over Turkish-style trousers, Lady Harberton described the item as 'a skirt, with trimmings as usual, only we have a skirt for each leg, and over this some drapery coming to below the knees, and arranged according to individual taste.'[22]

In May 1883, the Exhibition of the Rational Dress Society was held at Prince's Hall, Piccadilly Street, London. Its aim was to create a supply and demand by introducing the clothing trade to the appropriate types of clothes to sell and to encourage men and women to adopt them. As well as the exhibition, the society shared its beliefs via publications and lectures. Lady Harberton herself lectured in a divided skirt 'of rich black satin, and a cutaway coat of softest velvet, trimmed with lace and jet'.[23] A variation was the Wilson pattern divided skirt with 'no apparent division showed only a series of box pleats taken from waist to ankle. A short folded drapery was arranged in front, with long back drapery in outstanding pleats,' the trouser element was not too 'pronouncedly brought forward.'[24] So reported the *Aberdeen Evening News*, going on to say, 'Anything that looks like a desire to ape male attire is regarded with disfavour by every true woman, who, while she may be anxious to benefit her sex, sees the wisdom of guarding against the shafts of ridicule.'[25] A timely reminder of the ridicule that Amelia Jenks Bloomer suffered when she had tried to introduce her outfit over thirty-five years previously.

Other leading members of the Society were Constance Wilde (wife of Oscar) and Mary Haweis. According to the *Rational Dress Society Gazette* in 1889, they would protest,

against the introduction of any fashion in dress that either deforms the figure, impedes the movements of the body, or in any way tends to injure the health. It protests against the wearing of tightly-fitting corsets; of high-heeled or narrow toed boots and shoes; of heavily-weighted skirts, as rendering healthy exercise almost impossible; and of all tie down cloaks or other garments impeding on the movements of the arms. It protests against crinolines or crinolettes of any kind as ugly and deforming.…. The maximum weight of clothing (without shoes) approved by the Rational Dress Society, does not exceed seven pounds.[26]

The ideal outfit envisaged would allow freedom of movement, would weigh no more than is needed for warmth, would have no unnecessary pressure on any part of the body, and would not deviate too conspicuously from current fashion. They were far more concerned with the unhealthiness of modern fashions than any of the artistic ideals of both Artistic and Aesthetic societies.

Members of the society would give regular talks throughout the country on the pros of Rational Dress. Lady Harberton was described as a 'fluent and racy speaker and knows how to express logical arguments in a very forcible and racy manner'.[27] In 1889, Charlotte Carmichael Stopes (mother of Marie Stopes, founder of the first birth-control clinic in Britain) staged a coup at a meeting of the British Association for the Advancement of Science in the theatre of The Literary and Philosophical Society in Newcastle upon Tyne. Her impromptu talk on the tyranny of fashion and the need for Rational Dress was the biggest news from the meeting and was reported in newspapers throughout the country.

In the 1880s, more middle-class women started to take up jobs; they looked to live a healthier lifestyle which included regular exercise, the growth of women's movements and the strengthening push for greater equality all played a part in the gradual acceptance of what were looked on as radical changes in dress. Miss Ada Ballin predicted that 'Reform, to be effective, must be gradual and it takes some time for the public to become accustomed to a new idea, even in dress.'[28]

It took a change in attitude towards what was deemed acceptable behaviour for women in society but each of these movements, from the Artistic, through the Aesthetic and on to the Rational Dress movement, along with their associated personalities, sowed the seeds of the much less structured fashions that emerged in the twentieth century.

Fabrics and colours of the 1880s

Listed below are some of the most common fabrics and popular colours as recorded in fashion magazines, pattern books and adverts of the 1880s.

Algerian, angola, auvergnat velvet, batiste, beige, blonde, brocaded velvet, cambric, camel hair cloth, cashmere, chenille, Cheviot, China silk, coquille, corah silk (printed), cordeliere, corduroy velveteens, cotton (printed with dark backgrounds & large flowers & leaves), damask, duchesse satin, faille, foulard, gauze, Genoa velvet, ingrain cotton, linen, Louis velveteen, Madras, melton, merveilleuse, moiré, muslin, muslin-de-laine, nainsook, nankin, nun's veiling, Ottoman brocade, Ottoman silk, percales, pekin, plaid, plush, polarian cloth, pomelle, Pompadour cretonne, Pompadour sateen, Roxburghe cloth, sateen, satin, satinette, satin foulards, satin merveilleux, satin striped pekin, Scotch gingham, silk, serge, shot velvet, sicilienne, silk bourette, silk muslin, stamped velvet, stockinette, surah, tarlatan, tulle, tussore, Umritza, veiling, velveteen, vicuna, vigogne, washing silk, woollens, woollen reps, zephyr.

Almond, amber, apricot, art bronze, asparagus green, azalea red, beetroot red, beige, biscuit, black, blue, bluish gray, blush, bottle green, brown, bronze, bronze green, buttercup yellow, carbourier red, cardinal red, carnation, cerise, cherry, chestnut, china blue, chocolate, cinnamon, claret, coffee, coral, copper, copper brown, copper red, corn, cornflower blue, cream, crimson, crushed raspberry, crushed strawberry, dahlia red, dark blue, dark garnet, dark green, dark grenat, dark grey, dark maroon, dark nasturtium yellow, dark prune, dark red, deep ruby, dove grey, dull green, dull red, eau de Nil, écru, electric blue, elephant grey, Etna brown (a rich red brown), faded rose, fawn, ficelle, flax grey, flesh pink, Florence bronze, forest green, forget-me-not blue, fuchsia purple, fuchsia red, garnet, geranium red, gold, golden brown, grass green, green, grey, hair, heather, heliotrope, hop green, hunters green, hyacinth pink, iron grey, ivory, ivy green, jonquil, leaf brown, leather, leden grey, lemon, lichen green, lie de vin, light bluish grey, light brown, light bronze, light green, light nut brown, lilac, lizard green, lobelia blue, mahogany, maize, malachite green, marine blue, maroon, mascotte-brown, mastic, mauve, military blue, mineral blue, mineral green, moonlight blue, moss green, mouse, mushroom, myrtle green, nasturtium red, nasturtium yellow, Neapolitan sky blue, nut brown, oak, oatmeal, old copper, old gold, olive, olive green, orange, orchid purple-red, pale blue, pale nasturtium red, pale olive, pale pink, pansy, peacock blue, pearl grey, petunia, pine green, pink, polar blue, poppy red, primrose, prune, punch blue (a kind of slate blue), purple, red, reddish slate, reseda, rifle green, rose, rose pink, royal blue, ruby, rust, sage green, salmon pink, sand, sapphire blue, scarlet, sea green, seal brown, Sèvres blue, shell pink, silver grey, sky blue, slate, smoke grey, snuff, steel grey, straw, strawberry red, sulphur, sunflower yellow, sycamore, tea rose, terracotta, topaz, turquoise blue, turtle grey, tuscan, ultramarine blue, violet, wallflower brown, wallflower red, watercress green, white, willow green, wine, yellow.

A trio of ladies in large, heavily decorated hats and with more bouffant hair styles. Both are a precursor of the forthcoming Edwardian styles, c.1900.

Chapter 6

1890s

The previous decades of Victoria's reign are often readily identifiable by certain extremes of fashion. Huge crinoline skirts in the late 1850s and early 1860s, masses of false hair piled on the head in the 1870s and a sharp angular bustle protruding from the back in the 1880s. The 1890s were no different and would see their own distinctive fashions evolve and then disappear, as fashions are known to do, in this case when the bodice, particularly its sleeves, became the centre of attention.

The 1890s Look

At the end of the 1880s the bodice sleeve at the shoulder seam was starting to show an excess of fabric, sticking up vertically above the shoulder. This little 'puff' of fabric continued to inflate, reaching its greatest size around 1895–96, although sleeves generally remained tight from elbow to wrist throughout the decade. *The Woman at Home* describes the 'Montgolfiere' sleeve, which was 'two yards wide in circumference, forming an immense round balloon ending below the elbow'.[1] Other sleeves included the Italian sleeve with a full puff above the shoulder then tight to the wrist with a buttoned cuff; the double sleeve, comprising of a long, tight sleeve with a ballooning, loose over-sleeve down to the elbow, found mostly on summer outfits; and the demi-gigot, which was close fitting with a high shoulder.

The early 1830s had also seen large puffed sleeves known as 'gigot' sleeves, the name resurfaced in the 1890s, but the more descriptive 'leg-o-mutton' would also now be used in the vernacular for the style. As with the sleeves of the 1830s, those of the 1890s were often cut on the cross of the fabric and required internal cushions stuffed with eiderdown or stiffened muslin to hold their shape, they were also often made of a different material and colour to the bodice. Once they had reached their

The most distinctive aspect of the 1890s was the inflating then deflating of the sleeve. They reached their peak of fullness mid-decade, reducing to a puff at the top of the sleeve by the end.

maximum size, around 1896, they then started to deflate, becoming a neat puffball at the shoulder, with the rest of the arm in a tight-fitting sleeve which often extended over the hand, sometimes to a point. The much diminished puff could be frilled and the sleeve ruched or tucked down their length. Finally, by 1900, sleeves were straight and narrow again.

The bodice itself often contrasted with the skirt (sleeves could be the same colour and fabric as the latter) and could be fashioned in a number of ways. Early on, the front could have a crossover appearance, by the end of the decade (c.1898) it could be quite full and appear 'pouched', so it hung over the belt fastening at one side, it could be draped diagonally, with or without a yoke, the waistline could be defined by a pointed band, it could be gathered, frilled and even drawn over so it fastened at one side. No matter how loose it appeared to be, it was usually heavily boned. The first years of the decade saw a vertical emphasis with V-shaped trimmings or long narrow revers pointing down to a low waist. Lace frills and jabots were popular. Once the sleeves started increasing in size, so the decoration on the bodice changed to further emphasise the shoulder width. For example, reveres spread towards the shoulder as the sleeves widened and this, along with the increase in the width of the skirt hem, emphasised the small waist. Over the decade there were false square or rounded yokes, an effect achieved with the trimmings rather than construction, and later a pointed, upside down V-shaped yoke, a sailor collar or a high collar that splayed out a little.

With the disappearance of the bustle, skirts became much more fitted and smoother over the hips, even the residual hip pads vanished quite quickly. Skirts were now comparatively plain after decades of flounces, drapes and decoration, fitting closely to the hips and shaped by gores at the hem, some had between four and six, and fullness at the back. The 'umbrella' skirt was made from double width fabric cut on the cross, it had only the one seam which ran down the centre-back and was concealed by box pleats. It was fitted snugly to the waist using darts. By mid-decade there were numerous variations on this; the Marie Antoinette had a total of seven gores, one in front, two at each side and two at the back; the 'ripple' skirt had eleven very narrow gores and measured six and a half yards round; the Directiore skirt had seven gores, the four at the back being fluted. By the end of the decade the skirt was fitting closely to about knee level, then flared out to the ground.

A beautifully fitting dress in an unusual floral fabric, the sleeves are starting to expand, c.1893.

The sailor collar on the bodice was a fashionable look, sleeves have completely deflated and hats are becoming larger, c.1900.

It seemed that as the sleeves increased in width so did the skirt hemlines and like the crinoline at its height, some of these skirts were huge around the hem, *The Woman at Home* (1894) describes the 'rotonde' circular-shaped skirt which clung to the hips at the top, but by the time it reached the hem measured a good five yards. The following year a later edition explains that you can renovate an old skirt to gain this effect by inserting 'soufflets' or pleated fans to any depth you please as far as the knee. These may be surmounted by one or three tiny formal Louis Onze bows of velvet.'[2] In fact, readers of the magazine were often instructed on how to renovate older garments, in 1896 instructions were given on updating a blouse or bodice:

> sleeves can be covered with tiny frills or slashed at intervals, or in the middle only with crêpe or tulle…. Or the bodice may be opened at the front and have a vest of jet over white satin, pin-point velvet on spangled white tulle let in.[3]

The 1890s saw the further development of the 'tailor-made' outfit of jacket and skirt that had appeared in the previous decade, made from tweeds, corduroys, wools and serge for colder weather, and lighter fabrics such as crêpe de chine and wool muslin for summer. The former were often decorated with braid and velvet appliqué. In the early years the jacket was three-quarter-length with wide revers and big sleeves and often worn over a waistcoat and topped with a straw boater, the boaters in this decade having wider brims than those of the 1880s. *The Woman at Home* describes one such outfit as:

> composed of bright brown cloth, having the neck and under sleeves of a darker shade of velvet edged with fur. On the skirt are also two panels of velvet. Carved gold buttons finish this most charming arrangement, and a hat of brown velvet with gold and brown ribbons and yellow roses is well worn with it.[4]

The same magazine also mentions the fact that 'the size of buttons in ominously increasing; some of them are as large as small saucers.'[5]

Blouses (or 'shirts') became popular with the 'tailor-made', sporting a starched collar and a masculine-style tie, often seen with a pointed Swiss belt. By the mid-1890s the jacket was shorter. Blouses and ties also became a popular garment to wear with just a plain skirt, becoming widely accepted as informal daywear. Although they appeared loose-fitting, the blouse still had a boned lining.

Rational Dress in Sport and Work

Women continued to take up sporting activities. As tricycles evolved they became the far-more compact, cheaper and practical bicycles, their popularity increasing. In 1892 the Lady Cyclists Association was set up and was a keen advocate of the right to dress appropriately, believing cycling allowed women to escape the somewhat restrictive Victorian social norms. In 1896, cycling was all the rage in the London season and ladies' bicycle paperchases became popular. At these events one person was designated the 'hare' and everyone else 'hounds'. The 'hare' sets off leaving a trail of paper pieces for the rest to follow when they set off some time later. The 'hounds' have to catch the 'hare' before it reached the designated finishing point.

Companies that manufactured bicycles encouraged women to take up the hobby by producing specially adapted machines. To accommodate the conventional skirts cyclists could have open, drop, or step-through frames; likewise, guards were added to moving parts to prevent the fabric from snagging. Clothing was also adapted; cycling skirts, like walking skirts, were cut a few inches shorter, there were bifurcated skirts and long skirts with bloomers concealed underneath. But by far the most daring was the appearance of the tailored knickerbocker suit with its knee-length breeches, reminiscent of Amelia Bloomer's much lampooned outfit in the 1850s. Fabrics were hard wearing, often of tweeds and serge, and colours were greys, greens and brown, as they hid the dirt and dust the mainly unmetalled roads kicked up.

Some women adopted the knickerbocker outfit quickly, many more were a little more reticent. Sixteen-year-old Teresa 'Tessie' Reynolds wore such an outfit in 1893 when she set a record of eight hours and thirty-eight minutes cycling from Brighton to London and back. Adopting the 'rational' outfit ensured publicity for both Tessie and the Rational Dress Movement. *Bicycling News* that year reported:

Miss Reynolds sets an example, and so long as a lady can ride well and mount gracefully I see no objection at all to the adoption by her of a suitable, eminently rational, and particularly safe costume, which relieves her once and for all of the flapping and dangerous skirt, which catches the wind, impeded the free action of the limbs, and every now and then has a pleasing trick of getting mixed up with the machinery.[6]

Tessie continued to wear the outfit regularly after her world record.

Five years later Lady Harberton, one of the founders of the Rational Dress League, was refused service at the Hautboy Inn, Ockham, Surrey, for wearing a knickerbocker cycling costume. The landlady refused to let her go into the public coffee room, instead directing her to the bar. The incident made the national newspapers as she sued the landlady, albeit unsuccessfully. Sadly, although the outfit was practical, it was also still seen as controversial and wearers were considered to be stepping outside of accepted gender rules.

LADIES' "RATIONAL" DRESS

FOR

CYCLING.

OUR WORLD-FAMED SPECIALTY

THE "KNICKER-SKIRT,"

From **5/11,** Post Free.
SEPARATE LININGS, FROM **2/6.**

ILLUSTRATIONS AND PATTERNS SENT POST FREE.

THE IDEAL GARMENT FOR

FREEDOM, HEALTH, COMFORT.

IMPROVED MATERIALS FOR THIS SEASON.

SPÉCIALITÉ

HYGIENIC CORSETS and UNDERWEAR

FOR LADY CYCLISTS.

Illustrated Price Lists Post Free.

WM. SMALL & SON,

1 & 2, CHAMBERS STREET,
EDINBURGH.

Advert for the Rational Dress 'Knicker Skirt' for bicycling, c.1896.

For ladies who were not willing to wear the knickerbocker suit and run the risk of insult or injury when out on their bicycles, a number of suitably respectable and practical outfits were patented. In 1895, Alice Bygrave designed a skirt with a dual pulley system sewn into the front and rear seams. This allowed the wearer to adjust the length of the skirt to suit whatever activity she was doing. It was manufactured and distributed by Jaeger and sold throughout the UK and America. A year later, in 1896, Mary and Sarah Pease patented a cycling skirt and cape. The idea being that a cyclist could wear the skirt over their knickerbockers, removing it completely to cycle, it could then be worn as a cape or, using a gathering ribbon, be secured to the handlebars. The same year also saw Henrietta Müller patent her three-piece cycling suit, which consisted of a tailored jacket, a skirt that could be shortened using loops on the hem that fastened to buttons on the waistband, and a combined blouse and bloomer undergarment. She also realised lady cyclists would probably need pockets and included five in the outfit, but encouraged ladies to add more if they desired.

The changes in outerwear associated with the rational outfit required changes to underwear. Dr Jaeger recommended 'knitted' vests and pantaloons made from stockinette, as well as his Sanitary Woollen System corset. This was boned stockinette, so stretched more comfortably over the body and was less restricting than the traditional corset. Corsetry designed for sports was often fitted higher on the hips and was generally not so heavily boned, allowing more freedom of movement.

In the late nineteenth and early twentieth centuries, the bicycle and the rational dress associated with it came to symbolise the emerging 'New Woman', a more active an independent woman than had ever been seen before; one who was not only going out to work, but was also seeking to get the vote. Some who wore the new costume reported having rocks as well as insults hurled at them. Most female cyclists simply wanted a leisurely ride and didn't want to run the risk of abuse while out, or of being barred from hotels, and subsequently settled for the more socially acceptable long skirts.

Cycling was one of the most popular sports taken up by women but there were others that increased in popularity. Golf had been played by women for a number of years and clubs like St Andrews often had special areas for ladies to play and in 1893, the Ladies Golf Union was formed. Women golfed in skirts, *The Woman at Home* (1894) advised: 'golf gowns should be as light as possible, and that they should clear the ground by at least six inches'. It goes on to describe the ideal costume seen at St Andrews which 'was of fine black serge with a broad band of scarlet leather in the hem of the skirt. The scarlet blouse with full bishop's sleeves, was arranged in soft folds which would in no way interfere with the movements of its wearer.' The 1890s saw the introduction of 'golf jerseys'; these were made in ribbed stockinette and in 1895, Messrs Allison & Co. of Regent Street, sold them in 'plain colours and a variety of stripes. These jerseys fit beautifully to the figure, and are extremely neat and suitable for all outdoor games, on account of the ease and freedom of movement they afford the wearer.' They fastened on the left shoulder and under the arm and were priced at 10s 6d for plain and 18s 6d for striped. Although still worn over a corset they were much more

No. 6.

A knitted jersey 'blouse' and matching cap for 'golfing, tennis or on the river', *The Woman at Home*, 1895.

practical than a blouse and jacket, hand-knitted versions were also available.[7]

Swimming was also popular, but the decade saw little change to the one-piece bathing costume with over-skirt, or the two-piece suit of drawers and jacket which appeared in the 1880s. Necklines and sleeves did change, with the former becoming low and square and the latter, like other sleeves, becoming larger and more puffed. Legs were bare from the knees down till later in the decade, but black stockings gradually became the norm. The previously favoured straw hat gave way to mob caps to protect the hair as women became more serious about swimming. They were often made in jaconet (a lightweight cotton), twill, sateen and silk with a waterproof backing and came in colours such as pink, yellow, white, check and turkey-red.

The 1890s saw other sports increase in popularity; the Original English Lady Cricketers toured Great Britain between 1890 and 1892 playing exhibition matches, and the first international ladies field hockey match between Ireland and England was held in 1896 with Ireland winning 2–0. Participation in sporting activities was blossoming, and along with it a fashion for more appropriate, masculine inspired attire. *The Glasgow Evening Post* reported an event which caused quite a stir in London, the appointment of the first women gardeners at Kew by then Director William Thiselton-Dyer. Annie Gulvin and Alice Hutchins were the first female graduates from the Royal Horticultural College at Swanley, Kent, to gain appropriate employment. They were, however, due to their lack of experience, not allowed to be employed as 'gardeners', but were added to the books as 'boys' who would be fully trained by the gardeners. They were each paid 10s a week.

Thistleton-Dyer was a strict disciplinarian who had introduced uniforms for the gardeners, he expected the new recruits to wear the chosen outfit. Initial reports that the women had to wear trousers were soon labelled 'exaggerated', and it was clarified that they were to wear a uniform of a neat blue serge jacket, necktie, knickerbockers, gaiters and shoes when at work, 'as skirts might cause serious damage to valuable plants in the crowded house'.[8] Other reports claim that it was also to prevent their male colleagues from being distracted. They were provided with a room in which to change when going to and from work, although some newspaper reports state they covered their outfit with a long coat. The *South Wales Daily News* heralded it as 'another step towards the equalisation of the sexes'. Gulvin and Hutchins became something of a tourist attraction, but visitors were disappointed because they worked in a 'private' section of the garden not open to visitors.

The *Journal of the Kew Guild* voiced opinions that were, by and large, in favour of female gardeners stating:

> the experiment has so far proved satisfactory, and there does not appear to be any insuperable difficulty in the way of the adoption by women of gardening as a profession … .the work of certain departments in large establishments can no doubt be done as well by women as men.'[9]

However, the *Journal* does point out that marriage would terminate a woman's gardening career and that she could 'never attain to the rank of head-gardener and the enjoyment of £80 or £100 a year with a cottage, milk and vegetables … we do not see how any self respecting woman can hope to be a wife and mother and a gardener as well.'[10] By 1898 Alice Hutchins had been promoted to sub-foreman and Annie Gulvin had been replaced by Jessie Newsham and Florence Potter.

Foundation Garments

With the shape of the skirt totally changing, becoming a flowing A-line shape, once again under garments had to adapt. Petticoats also became fitted round the hips and flared at the hem to help support the new shape of skirt and additional help was given by the bottom ten inches or so of the skirt being stiffened with horsehair or other such interlining. This was enough to produce the desired silhouette. Silk became a popular choice for petticoats, as *Woman and Home* would note, 'petticoats are being made in all the good houses without which the new dress is a failure; to obviate weight, as they are very full, they are made of thin silk, lined with nun's veiling'.[11]

The corset was still a necessity if you wanted to achieve the desired shape, there were now even adverts targeting particular consumer groups. The 'Pretty Housemaid' corset was aimed specifically at women in domestic service, having a busk protector to stop it breaking due to all the required bending. However, attitudes to corsetry were gradually starting to change, while very few women were willing to discard them completely they were becoming more open to changes in the garment. There was a growing awareness that corsetry was not necessarily a good thing, *Woman at Home* announced that 'slender waists are on the wane', and advised that corsets were:

> usually made too hard and allowed to meet in the back, where they ought to give full play and ventilation to the spine by being kept well apart. Girls should really not wear corsets at all until they reach the age of seventeen, unless they can have them perfectly made to order, and graduated to suit each year that brings them closer to womanhood.

The same magazine tells of Paris Mignonne belts, described as 'miniature corsets just to hold in the waist and slightly support the bust; they do not lace, they simply strap across the back and fasten in front under a hook, and can be put on in a moment.'[12]

The increased uptake of sporting activities among women also helped change attitudes to the corset as new designs were created to give support but make movement easier. The Aertex Cellular Clothing Company developed a breathable corset in the mid-1890s shaped to allow freedom of movement for sports. Made from the mesh Aertex fabric it has a busk at the front and lacing at the back with twelve sets of double bones inserted into tapes and stitched onto the fabric.

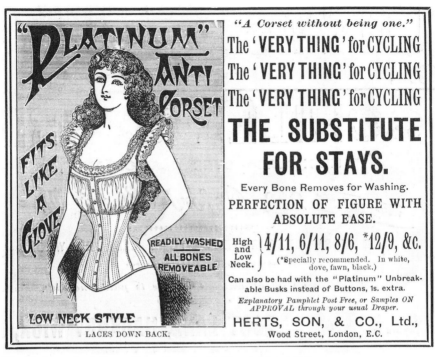

The Platinum Anti-Corset for cycling, *Lady's Pictorial*, July 1897.

Unlike the majority of corsets it is cut to sit under the bust and above the hips, curving up and down to points centre front and back. Other 'healthy' corsets, known as 'ventilated' corsets, were made from a base of horizontal cotton tapes about an inch apart. Onto these were stitched the vertical boning channels, spaced to give the correct shape. The spaces between the boning tapes and the horizontal cotton tapes were intended to allow air to circulate, the skin to breathe and perspiration to evaporate.

Even without the added strain of sporting activity on a corset, they were generally only expected to last about twelve months. The bones, particularly in areas of the most strain, could bend, snap and either poke through clothing or dig into the wearer's flesh. Some corsets were sold with replacement bones allowing repairs to be carried out at home, although many of the places that sold corsetry also offered repair and cleaning services. In 1893, the Oktis Corset Shield appeared in drapers shops, promising to double the life of a corset. Made of flat bones covered in calico, it was tacked onto the inside of the corset to reinforce the sides of the waist where the bones were under the most stress. They were described in *The Gentlewoman Magazine* as:

> a real boon to womankind … they do not add to the size of the waist, and they prevent that ugly bend which comes in the corset after it has been worn a few times. The Oktis Shields are made of zairoid, a whalebone like substance which is absolutely rustless, and cannot stain the underwear if damp from perspiration.[13]

The 1890s favoured a more generous bust and for those ladies wishing to enhance their assets, various stuffings and pads were improvised and garments were manufactured with uplifting and padded linings. In the late 1890s the Lemon Cup Bust improve was advertised. The Symington Corset collection describes them as:

> From outside this garment resembles two circular pads contained within a simple white cotton pouch. Inside, the pads reveal that they contain a light, coiled spring packed into a pad of bleached horsehair. The springs are anchored onto strips of whalebone that run horizontally. When the garment was pinned over a corset, or onto a chemise/camisole, the bust would push the whalebones into a deep outward curve and force the spring out into the pad to give the impression of a larger, more generous bust.[14]

If such a contraption was not your thing then another, simpler way of enhancing the bust was to use a frilled improver. This is simply a heavily ruffled and starched panel that sat across the bust over the corset and its cover. The intensity of the ruffles could be adjusted by gathering tapes that could be tightened or released as wished.

For other items of underwear there were few, if any, radical changes of design. The 'Deeanjay' Combination was made of silk and wool mixed and had woven seams 'like a superior made stocking' and claimed 'to be shaped on highly scientific principles, and is beautifully finished, and being ribbed and very pliable, fits closely to the figure, producing the greatest possible amount of comfort.' The advert goes on to claim 'the hygienic properties of silk and wool combined are well known and are highly commended by the faculty as a preventative against rheumatism.'[15]

Adverts for suspender belts were also becoming more common, the 'Warren Hose Supporter' being one, although towards the end of the nineteenth century elastic suspenders were being attached to the bottom of the corsets. One interesting item that appears in adverts from 1899 is the Portia Combined Stocking Suspender and Shoulder Support, described in its advertising as 'Adaptable to any figure by adjustment of centre clip. For use during cycling, tennis, golfing, sculling and in gymnasium; also recommended for those with round shoulders and contracted chest.'[16] From the very basic drawing included in the advert, this looks like two large loops joined at the back through which your arms go. From under the arm hangs the suspender straps which split into two at stocking height, attaching to the stocking tops at the sides of the leg. An interesting idea, though I'm not sure how comfortable it would be. As for stockings, these were now available in an array of colours and designs; in 1894 an advert for Peter Robinson of Oxford Street, London, mentions 'pure silk hose, black and 75 shades',[17] and advertises diagonal stripes, fancy fronts, fancy stripes and patterned cycling and golfing hose, available in silk and lisle. However, black was the most popular, and practical, colour for everyday wear, although these too were often decorated with inserts, patterns and even embroidery.

One interesting article in the *Grantham Journal* from August 1895 tells the tale of three young ladies who had been caught smuggling lace. They had been making a couple of trips a week across to France, which the port authorities found a little suspicious, so on one return trip they were taken aside, questioned and searched. Nothing was found, although it was noted that their petticoats and undergarments were trimmed with the loveliest lace. Still convinced something was not quite right, the English authorities arranged to have them searched on their next arrival in France, their underwear was quite plain. They were followed to a house where they stayed all day and on landing back in England were searched again. This time their underwear was covered in yards of expensive French lace, five or six rows on each petticoat. Other similar stories tell of false busts and India rubber hip pads being used to smuggle alcohol.

"Prevents Hair Falling!"

KOKO FOR THE HAIR

Awarded Diploma, American Exhibition, London, 1887.

Some stimulant is absolutely necessary to be used upon the head, particularly when the hair commences to fall off, no matter what the age, or it will continue to fall. Every hair preparation advertised is not safe to use; some are good for the hair, and some are positively injurious. It is therefore necessary to select one for use that is known to be perfectly safe. During the continuance of the American Exhibition, the public had an opportunity of seeing each day for six months, at our stall (a view of which is given above), some half-a-dozen young ladies with splendid hair of every shade of colour, from very fair to black, who used KOKO FOR THE HAIR freely every day, **used no other dressing**, and whose hair was always in the best possible condition. This is **proof positive** that KOKO FOR THE HAIR is not only entirely safe, but is also the best dressing that can be used on the hair. It contains no grease nor oil, and leaves the hair in the best possible condition, increases its growth, and entirely prevents it from falling out.

'Koko for the Hair', advert from *The Woman at Home*, 1895.

Accessories

Until the mid-1890s hair was still worn pulled back from the face in a neat chignon, high upon the back or even on the top of the head. However, *The Woman at Home* advised that this did not suit everyone as it was 'hard and unbecoming to most faces'. Instead they recommend the newer, softer look:

> the hair worn rather loose and slightly raised in front with a few side curls is far prettier; sometimes a frisette is used to give height

Dorothy Peaps, the width of the sleeves is emphasized by the addition of epaulettes, c.1895.

to the hair in front, but it is still much better to curl the front hair back every night. This will give it a natural wave that will keep it in order.[18]

This less severe, more relaxed look would last throughout the decade, a precursor to the famous bouffant 'Gibson Girl' look that became extremely popular in the early twentieth century.

While the small hats from the 1880s remained fashionable, hats now came in all shapes and sizes:

Vera, Gladys, Linda and Chris Leslie, Tynemouth, September 1893.

silk beavers, either soft or as hard as a gentleman's silk hat, are fashionable in fawn, grey or black. Large plumes of ostrich tips are grouped at the back, while a few rosettes of the new flora or Indian velvet ribbon adorn the front. There are picture hats, round hats, and compact demure felt hats trimmed with rooster's feathers.[19]

There were also velvet hats, sailor style hats, toques and beefeater shapes in mixed straws; 'they can be trimmed with a large brown or black velvet bow at the back and a flounce of cream lace over the brim, which should have an aigrette of flowers on the left side, which can be changed to suit the seasons or your own toilette.'[20]

The year 1896 saw a short-lived popular fashion for a very broad ribbon tied around the crown of a hat that was fastened in a large bow at the back. Ladies who were handy with a needle and thread were using old handkerchiefs and lappets from the now out of fashion indoor caps to create bows to adorn their hats. And when the upper body was at its widest due to the enormous sleeves, the look was often balanced out with wide-brimmed hats. One of the most popular fashions towards the end of the decade was borrowed from the male wardrobe, this was the straw boater and was often seen with the 'tailor-made' and remained in fashion till about the 1930s. Whatever the style, the hat was nearly always perched rather high and straight on the head.

One thing that remained constant was the profusion of decoration applied to the hats, *Woman at Home* (1894) noted:

> Hats have this autumn launched forth extravagantly; they are mostly trimmed with tulle, birds and flowers. Rustic shapes are draped with the brightest chiffon, and the new slender birds with curved wings of every hue are universally used.[21]

The article also goes on to say that 'We may comfort ourselves on humanitarian principles that these winged creatures are not "born, but made", for we never saw a specimen of the feathered tribe that quite resembles them.' We can but hope these were indeed manufactured ornamentation but the wearing of feathers, birds wings and even full stuffed birds on hats was nothing new and seemed to gather pace in the 1890s.

The Fin, Fur and Feather Folk amalgamated with The Plumage League in 1891 to form the Society for Protection of Birds (SPB), that gained its Royal charter in 1904. Originally having an all female membership who campaigned against the fashion for wearing exotic feathers, they swore to refrain from wearing the feathers of any bird not killed for food (for some reason the ostrich was an exception), to actively discourage the destruction of birds and work towards their protection. London was the international centre of the plumage trade. In 1892 a single order of feathers by a London dealer amounted to 6,000 birds of paradise, 40,000 hummingbirds and 360,000 various East Indian bird feathers.[22]

One of the most popular feather trimmings in this decade were the 'osprey' or 'aigrette' feather. Actually coming from an egret rather than an osprey, the London feather trade required six egrets to yield one ounce of plumes. By the turn of the century the egret was virtually extinct in North America and numerous other birds were approaching that point due to what became known as 'murderous millinery' in the press. In 1897 W.H. Hudson, a representative of the SPB, witnessed the sale of 80,000 parrots and 1,700 Birds of Paradise skins, describing the size of the haul thus: 'Spread out in Trafalgar Square they would have covered a

Shorter capes became popular to accommodate the bustle, this one is worn with the simpler gored skirt, c.1890.

large proportion of that space with a grass-green carpet, flecked with vivid purple, rose and scarlet.'[23]

It wasn't just fancy tropical birds that suffered at the hands of the milliners. Indigenous British birds such as herons, Great Crested Grebes, Kittiwakes and gulls all fell victim over the decades as they were culled to decorate the hats and bonnets of the fashionable woman. Sadly, the trade in tropical birds to adorn hats and other fashionable items would not reach its peak till the first decade of the twentieth century, but the numbers used in the 1890s were still staggering

Outerwear was generally dictated by the size of the sleeve. Initially you could find long cloaks with high collars and concealed arm-slits, as well as both three-quarter and short cloaks. As sleeves grew in size they influenced the style of outdoor wear. Coats with equally large sleeves were popular, but short hip-level capes proved to be the most practical for the huge bodice sleeves. These could have two or three tiers, be yoked, some had two straps that buttoned across the chest, or simply be wide and plain with a high, wired Medici collar. Messrs Swann & Edgar of Regent Street, London, in 1895 designed a 'cape made in green box cloth and ornamented with black cloth appliqué. It is three quarter circular shape and hangs in graceful folds around the figure.[24] As sleeves deflated jackets became possible again, variations included fur edging, yokes and collars, some with revers and some without.

Jewellery

The 1890s saw a return to small delicate pieces with a preference for stones with little or no colour such as opals, diamonds, pearls and moonstones.

Brooches of various motifs became popular such as horse racing, sailing ships, frogs, insects, owls, flowers and lizard, and the increased interest in sporting activities led to appropriate motifs such as rackets, balls and clubs. These could be worn on the bodice or pinned to the hat. Brooches also displayed girls' names, and the word 'Mizpah' became popular, a Hebrew word loosely translated as 'may God watch over you'. A sautoir (neck chain) fell well below the waist but was tucked into the waistband or attached to a brooch on the bodice. More unusual components were also used for special occasions, 'a throatlet is made of two rows of sable tails with rosettes of cream satin and long ends of lace falling on either side; a bunch of violets can be pinned to this'.

Fabrics and colours of the 1890s

Listed below are some of the most common fabrics and popular colours as recorded in fashion magazines, pattern books and adverts of the 1890s

Alpaca, barège, bengaline, bouclé, broché, cambric, cashmere, chiffon, cotton velvet (plain, flecked), crêpe de chine, crêpon (plain, shot, striped, floral) corduroy, cheviot, delaines, flowered brocade, foulard, grenadine, hopsack, jaconas, linen, merino, Merv, mohair, moiré (plain, with broché flowers and buds), mousseline de laine, mousseline de soie, muslin, pongee silk, poult de soie, satin, pompadour muslin, satin de laine, serge, silk (checked, figured, shepherds plaid, flowered, shot, chintz, with wavy lines and scattered flowers), surah, taffeta, tattersall, tulle, tweed, velvet (plain, shot, glacé), velveteen, vicuna, vigogne, voile, woollens, zephyr.

Almond green, amber, amethyst, apple green, apricot, arsenic green, biscuit, black, blotting paper pink, blush pink, bottle green, bright green, brown, buff, burnt sienna, butcher blue, butter, cerise, cherry, cherry rose, chestnut, coral, cornflower blue, crimson, dahlia, dark brown, dark grey, dove, deep red, deep rose, eau-de-nil, ecru, electric blue, emerald, eminence, fawn, flamingo, geranium pink, gold, golden brown, grass, green, grey, grey blue, heliotrope, lavender blue, laurel green, lemon, lichen green, lilac, maize, magenta, mauve, mignonette-green, mushroom, mustard, navy blue, olive green, orange, pale gold, pale grey, pale pink, pale rose, pale yellow, parchment, parma mauve, peach, peach-mauve, pearl grey, periwinkle, petunia, mother of pearl, old rose, pink, plum, primrose, prune, purple, red, reed green, rose pink, royal blue, salmon pink, sapphire, scarlet, sea green, silver white, slate grey, soft blue, steel blue, straw, sulphur yellow, terra-cotta, tartan, turquoise, violet, white, yellow.

Maggie Storey, Cullercoats fisher-girl. Note the multiple tucks on her black flannel 'perriket' to give weight and insulation, c.1898.

Chapter 7

Working Women

Throughout the Victorian age more and more women went to work, but there would be certain conventions concerning the areas where women could find employment. It was frowned upon and indeed considered 'not the done thing' for women of noble birth, landed gentry and the upper classes to work in any gainful employment although many did get involved in charity work and politics.

Those from the middle classes could work in what was considered to be a 'respectable' occupation, such as schoolteacher, governess, accounts' workers and even telephone operators. Lower-middle-class and upper-working-class women could find work as dressmakers, quality seamstresses, shop girls, cashiers, typists and secretaries, or working in family businesses such as drapery, haberdashers and milliners, smart grocery stores where a feminine touch was often a key to the success of the business were also acceptable.

The majority of working-class women were employed in textile mills, laundries and factories, making a huge range of items from boots and shoes to hats, tinned goods, confectionery, brushes and matches. However, once these ladies married, no matter their class, it was an accepted convention that they would give up work and raise a family, with their husband as the main provider. For the majority of these jobs, the women would go to work in their own clothes but would be provided with white aprons if the work required it.

Girls who were employed as domestic servants or cooks would originally have to provide their own working outfits, as Isabella Beeton advise in her new edition of *The Englishwoman's Cookery Book* (1867):

Be clean in your person, paying particular attention to the hands, which should always be clean.

Do not go about slipshod. Provide yourself with good well fitting boots. You will find them less fatiguing in a warm kitchen than loose untidy slippers.

Provide yourself with at least a dozen good-sized serviceable cooking aprons with bibs. These will save your gowns and keep you neat and clean.

As the century progressed and the households employing servants grew more affluent, uniform smartness of their servants became a projection of their own affluence and status, and staff would be provided with their workings clothes, aprons and caps of the approved style adopted by the house. Any damage to the servant's uniform could be stopped out of wages. Servant girls would usually have an afternoon off once a week, usually a Sunday afternoon, but they would have to wear their own clothes if they left the house on their own time.

As girls enjoyed a better standard of education, particularly after the 1870 Foster Education Act, hospitals began to engage in the formal training of nurses. One of the leading lights in this was Eva Lückes, the woman who would be Matron of The London Hospital from 1880 to 1919 and who published her training lectures in book form in 1884 under the title of *General Nursing*. Matron Lückes worked with Dr Frederick Treves to redesign the nurses' uniforms at the hospital. Treves is the surgeon known to modern history as the physician who cared for Joseph Merrick, unkindly named The Elephant Man, but in his day he was renowned for his surgical treatment of appendicitis and had published *The Dress of the Period in its Relation to Health* in 1884. His particular concern for the apparel of the nurses was the freedom of movement required to carry out their duties.

As a direct result, rigid corsets were not permitted and those

Domestic servants, their dresses are similar but not identical, their aprons and hats are the same and would have been issued by their employer, c.1894.

Nurse, note the white cuffs which would be removable to enable cleaning, c.1896.

worn by the nurses were adapted to allow more movement. The number of bones were reduced and those that were used were of a flexible steel. This style of corset was also popular with women engaged in sporting activities and would soon begin to permeate into wider society. Treves and Lückes also designed the nurses' dresses on rational lines in resilient cotton linen union fabrics capable of withstanding regular laundering at high temperatures. The designs and colours of the nurses' dress fabrics and the caps they wore would also delineate their place within the hierarchy of the nursing staff.

Women were not permitted to serve in the fighting forces, nor in the police at this time, so there were very few roles that involved women in uniform, although there were two notable exceptions. The 1823 Gaol Act had introduced wide-ranging reforms, including the the provision of female warders for female prisoners. The problem was, the Act did not have the legislation behind it to ensure it was enforced and so the recruitment, regulation and uniform of female wardresses did not take place in many prisons until after the 1880s. Prison wardresses tended to be given a more flexible uniform code, so rather than being the standard issue military-style tunic worn by male warders, the main stipulation was that the dresses supplied to wardresses should be midnight blue, black or dark brown in colour, each prison would usually stipulate a particular colour to be adopted by all wardresses working within it.

In the 1890s the standard wardress uniform consisted of skirt and bodice separates, with button fronts and leg-o-mutton sleeves. The bodice was pin-tucked and worn with a heavily boned corset underneath, all was made in black linen union (similar to those worn by nurses). On their head would be worn a toque-style bonnet tied under the chin with a satin ribbon. Women warders would also wear leather belts with simple, plain buckles, from which they wore keys on chains; some had pouches similar to the men, while others simply had their keys exposed and hooked onto their belts or left hanging like a chatelaine.

The other uniform worn by women in the Victorian era came along in the 1880s with the creation of The Salvation Army. At the time there was no formal uniform for members, just guidance that they should wear modest clothing suitable for a military organisation.

Salvation Army, a demure uniform topped by a strong straw bonnet with a blue ribbon to protect them from missiles, c.1884.

Prison wardress, one of the few women's uniforms at the time. It would be black and the end of the chain would carry their keys, c.1894.

Their work began on the streets and in the tenements of the East End of London where the Salvation Army women became known as 'Slum Saviours' and the 'Cellar, Gutter and Garret Brigades'. Much good work was done saving fallen women, succouring the sick and helping improve child care. However, the Salvation Army also vociferously opposed 'The

Demon Drink', and when their bands marched down streets on Sundays their opponents (some of them paid to do so by brewery owners) pelted the men and women on parade with stones and effluvia from the street. To protect their faces Salvation Army women were issued their first real item of uniform: strong black straw bonnets trimmed with a blue ribbon.

In the countryside, fashions would often be rather behind the times, some of the more remote rural areas maintaining a particular style of local dress decades after the period normally associated with it. At harvest time everyone, including girls and women, would lend a hand with the harvest and the picking of soft fruits. Everyday clothes in the countryside would be more hard wearing than those of the city and town folks. Country women would usually have aprons they kept aside for field work and would wear soft cotton sun bonnets with flaps to protect their necks from sunburn while bending over at their labours, reminiscent of the bavolet at the back of the bonnet.

As coastal areas became popular holiday destinations in the latter-half of the nineteenth century, the rustic charm of fisher-girls and fishwives from fishing communities became the subject of photographic studies and

Harvest time, note the aprons and soft cotton sun bonnets with a bavolet at the back to protect the neck from sunburn, c.1899.

as a result are probably the best recorded group of working women during the Victorian era. On the coast of Northumberland at Newbiggin and Cullercoats, women's outfits consisted of a black wool flannel 'bedgoon', or bedgown, for the upper-half of the body. This was a 'T' shaped jacket worn in crossover fashion and tied across the chest with tapes, with a silk or fabric square to fill the neckline. They would also have a colourful printed linen blouse for Sundays and best. On top of their 'bedgoon' they would wear a knitted or crocheted fringed shawl of grey or black wool, wrapped over the body and tucked in the waistband of the skirt.

The skirts, often referred to as petticoats or 'perrikets', were also made from the same black flannel but were particularly distinctive. They were worn just above the ankle and even as high as mid-calf to keep the hem out of sand and water on the beach, reduce wear and tear and allow free movement. The skirts were fastened with tapes at the back of the waist, but their most distinctive feature was the multiple rows of tucks running around the bottom of the skirt. The local belief was the more tucks the more stylish the skirt, but this also added weight and insulation; worn with an apron, sometimes made out of an old coat, they combined to make both practical working clothes and offered some protection from the chill winds of the North East coast. Very few of the younger girls wore a hat or a head covering as they worked, just pulled their shawls over their heads in bad weather. The older ladies had black and blue straw bonnets tied by ribbons or strings.

Photographs of those who had the least in society are seldom found in family albums, but they are not entirely without recorded images. People of all classes can take to criminal activity, but those having the hardest of times and those at their lowest ebb are particularly vulnerable. Those who were convicted of crimes and were admitted to prison had photographs taken for their criminal record. These images provide a remarkable archive of the clothes – mends and rips and all – of some of the poorest people.

The records of crime can also shine a light on the darkest corners of society. The most infamous crime of all occurred during the autumn of 1888; a series of murders ascribed to a still unidentified killer – Jack the Ripper. The body of Ripper victim Annie Chapman was discovered early in the morning of 8 September 1888, in the back yard of 29 Hanbury Street. At the inquest the jury viewed her corpse at the mortuary; the mutilations were concealed, but her clothing and a few tragic effects were also inspected and were listed. If you have ever wondered what it really meant to have only the clothes you stood up in, her tragic story is told through her clothes and effects:

- A long black figured coat that came down to her knees
- A black skirt
- Brown bodice
- Another bodice
- 2 petticoats
- A large pocket worn under the skirt and tied about the waist with strings (empty when found)
- Lace-up boots
- Red-and-white striped woollen stockings
- Neckerchief, white with a wide red border
- Scrap of muslin
- One small tooth comb
- One comb in a paper case
- Scrap of envelope containing two pills bearing the seal of the Sussex Regiment post marked 'London, 28, Aug., 1888'

Ready for Jack the Ripper, *The Illustrated Police News*, 22 September 1888.

The *Illustrated London News* of 22 September 1888 graphically illustrated the crimes and gave over the main section of their front cover to the Annie Chapman murder, illustrating how women were arming themselves with daggers, pistols and cudgels to protect themselves from the killer. Fear was not just limited to the East End, there were instances of Ripper scares all over Britain and women took to sewing convenient extra pockets into their skirts to carry some means of protection. Some also bought patent whistles to raise alarm if they were attacked.

Police experimented with officers dressing as women and loitering on streets in the East End in attempts to draw out and capture the killer. There were a small number, but two clearly recorded decoys were Detective Sergeant Robinson, who took to the streets in 'veil, skirt and petticoats', with Detective Sergeant Mather, who remained in his plain clothes.

Further ingenious suggestions for the apprehension of Jack the Ripper and appliances to be worn about the neck to prevent his deadly attack of were proffered, Mr W.H. Spencer summed up this theme in a letter printed in *The Star* on 2 October 1888:

a few young men of somewhat feminine appearance should be got up in disguises as females. They should wear around their necks steel collars made after the style of a ladies' collaret, coming well down the breast and likewise well down the back. My reason for this is … that the assassin first severs his victim's windpipe, thereby preventing her raising an alarm.

This lady is in full mourning, note the heavy black bracelets and black veil pushed to the back of the bonnet. This would be brought forward over the face when outside, c.1863.

Chapter 8

Mourning

Formal mourning etiquette was already established among the middle and upper classes by the time King William IV died on 20 June 1837. The following day a period of mourning was declared and was announced in national and provincial newspapers: 'it is expected that all persons, upon the present occasion of the death of his late Majesty, of blessed and glorious memory, do put themselves into decent mourning; and said mourning to begin upon Saturday, the 24 instant.'[1]

Public mourning was to cease on 3 August; for the Court it was to be carried on until 14 September. Many newspapers reported on the public's mourning, claiming it was deep and respectful, the *Cambridge Chronicle* which expounded:

> No class of lace, blond, or fancy article is adopted to relieve the sombre appearance; and notwithstanding the heat of the weather, heavy black bonnets, with deep crape trimmings, are used in the fashionable circles. In fact, the costume in society is more like family mourning than mere compliance with Court etiquette.[2]

When Albert died in December 1861, the queen, and the country, went into mourning. On 16 December, the Lord Chamberlain issued orders for the Full Mourning of the court: 'The Ladies attending Court to wear black woollen Stuffs, trimmed with Crape, plain Linen, black Shoes and Gloves, and Crape Fans. The Gentlemen attending Court to wear black Cloth, plain Linen, Crape Hatbands, and black Swords and Buckles.'[3]

It was later announced that on the 27 January 1862 Second Mourning would commence: 'the Ladies to wear black Silk Dresses, trimmed with Crape, and black Shoes and Gloves, black Fans, Feathers, and Ornaments. The Gentlemen to wear black Court Dress, with black Swords and Buckles, and plain Linen.'[4]

Half Mourning started on the 17 February and it was announced that 'The Ladies to wear black Dresses, with white Gloves, black or white Shoes, Fans, and Feathers, and Pearls, Diamonds, or plain Gold or Silver Ornaments. The Gentlemen to wear black Court Dress, with black Swords and Buckles.'[5]

Court mourning for Prince Albert finally ended on 10 March 1862, almost three months after his death. Victoria, however, wore black and half mourning for the rest of her life, although gradually her outfits became more elaborate, decorated with black beads and other trims.

The Etiquette of Mourning

Throughout the nineteenth century many families were large and lives were short, people became used to death and its traditions from an early age but as the century progressed, especially after the passing of Prince Edward, mourning was perceived as the 'decent thing' to be done, and in quite some style. The local builders and wheelwrights who made the coffins no longer dealt directly with the relatives of the deceased; they were replaced by 'front men' in veiled top hats and frock coats to undertake the family's wishes for the final farewell to the dearly departed. The undertaker was very much a creation of the Victorians. There would be mourning, black clothes and black-trimmed stationery, jet jewellery and glass-sided hearses pulled by horses with black plumes, and monuments of life-sized, hand-clasped, winged angels looking skyward, the funeralia of the late nineteenth century as phenomena has been described by historians as the 'Victorian celebration of death'.[6]

Beeton's *Housewife's Treasury of Domestic Information* described the stages of mourning:

The first sign to the outer world that one of a home circle is 'smitten by the common stroke of death', is the closing of the blinds at the windows of the house and the non-appearance in public of the female members of the family.[7]

From here the household would follow the acceptable rules of mourning, although these were complicated and often changed; consequently many turned to etiquette manuals, domestic manuals and ladies magazines for advice.

The various stages of Victorian mourning dictated what you could wear and how you could behave, all of which was dependant on a hierarchy of how close, or distant, the relationship with the deceased was. Upon the death of a family member the entire household was expected to go into mourning, including children and servants. The etiquette of mourning extended to step-parents, aunts, uncles, nieces, nephews, first and second cousins, friends and even servants. Each different circumstance followed the three phases of mourning, varying in duration, what had to be worn – or even skipping a phase completely depending on the relationship to the deceased. A married woman was expected to mourn her husband's relatives as she would hers, and even a second wife was expected to wear slight mourning for three months on the death of the parent of the first wife, but a widow had to endure the longest period or mourning of all.

For a widow, Full (also called First or Deep) Mourning lasted for one year and one day. Dresses were black, made from a dull fabric such as bombazine, a blend of silk and wool or cotton, and 'covered completely with crape'. Only black jet, or lookalike black jewellery in vulcanite or glass were allowed. When outside, a widow would wear heavy black crape veils attached to black hats and bonnets; attending social events was forbidden, only church services and family visits were allowed as *The Queen* magazine pointed out: 'Seclusion prescribed as imperative to be observed by a widow was one year, as far as the smallest social function was concerned, while large gatherings, including balls, were not attended until an additional nine months had elapsed.'[8]

Then came Second Mourning, lasting nine months, when crêpe was reduced to trimming the black dress. Finally Half Mourning for a further six months introduced

The touch of white at the neck and cuffs indicates that this lady is in half mourning, c.1872.

certain colours such as grey, lavender, mauve and white, initially as trims on the black dress. Gold, silver and gemstones could be added to, but not replace, the black jewellery. Many older women followed the example set by Victoria and chose to remain in mourning for the remainder of their lives, and the quality and extent of the mourning wardrobe proclaimed social status.

In 1881 *Sylvia's Home Journal* listed the recommended wardrobe for a new widow:

- One best dress of Paramatta covered entirely with crêpe.
- One dress, either a costume of Cyprus crape, or an old black dress covered with rainproof crape.
- One Paramatta mantle lined with silk, and deeply trimmed with crape.
- One warmer jacket of cloth lined and trimmed with crape.
- One bonnet of best silk crape with long veil.
- One bonnet of rainproof crape, with crape veil.
- Twelve collars and cuffs of muslin or lawn, with deep hems.
- One black stuff petticoat.
- Four pairs of black hose, either silk, cashmere or spun silk.
- Twelve handkerchiefs with black borders, for ordinary use, cambric.
- Twelve of finer fabric for better occasions.
- Caps either of lisse, tulle, or tarlatan, shape depending much upon age; young widows wear chiefly the Marie Stuart shape, but all widows' caps have long streamers. A good plan to buy extra streamers and bows.
- Summer parasol of silk, deeply trimmed with crape, almost covered with it, but no lace or fringe for the first year. Afterwards mourning fringe might be put on.
- Muff of Paramatta, and trimmed with crape.
- No ornaments, except jet, for the first year.
- Furs are not admissible in widows' first mourning, though very dark sealskin and astrachan can be worn when dress is changed.

Towards the end of Victoria's reign the attitude towards such strict mourning procedures started to relax a little. An article in *The Queen* in

February 1900 talks about a 'material change' in the laws of mourning and suggests it could be down to the large death toll of the war in South Africa which started in 1879, and the 'the prevalence of influenza in our midst'. This meant there were shorter periods of mourning and less time spent shut away from society. A widow could choose how much crape she could wear, some discarding it completely, or wearing it 'fancifully arranged', and could abandon it completely after six months. Likewise, the heavy crape veil was replaced by shorter ones of crape lisse and worn only for a very short period of time, or again discarded completely. As far as seclusion for the widow was concerned, three months became the upper limit after which time she would gradually reintroduce herself to society, but avoiding balls for a year. It was very much the younger generation setting these new trends, as elderly widows generally clung to old traditions

For a daughter mourning her father, according to *Sylvia's Home Journal* (1879), Full Mourning lasted seven months, again the dress would be dull black and heavily covered in black crêpe trim. Second Mourning lasted six months and involved no crape. Half Mourning, lasted another three months and permitted the wearing of grey, lavender, mauve and white trims on black garments. It was understood that she should give up all society engagements for at least four months and balls and dances for at least six. The approved time for mourning a parent didn't change much by 1900, although the Half Mourning period for little girls now started after six months rather than ten. The amount of crape worn for the first six months did reduce, either being disposed of completely or worn as a light trimming, and the withdrawal from society reduced to six weeks, with the exception of balls and dances which were to be avoided for three months. The mourning of a brother or sister was of six months' duration, three in crape, two in black and one in half mourning. By 1900 it was acceptable to mourn for four months in crape, two months in black, although crape was giving way to plain black and bows of crape on the bonnet or a band on the collar, accepting social invitations was allowed after three to six weeks depending on their nature.

As the 1880s progressed, the rituals of mourning were becoming less fashionable, although conventions were still observed by most. The changes in attitude to mourning are nicely illustrated in a feature in *The Queen* in 1898 entitled 'The Latest Authorities in the Correct periods of Ladies' Mourning', particularly for distant relatives. The article highlighted the latest acceptable approaches to mourning as advised by some of the leading ladies' magazines of the day, and it is interesting to see that they do differ in some instances. For example, a granddaughter mourning a grandparent should, according to Madge's *Manners for Women*, wear crape for three months, then black for two months, however *The Queen* was of the opinion that mourning should be worn for nine months. Similarly, a cousin mourning a cousin was advised by *Ladies Home* to be in mourning for one month, but *Illustrated London News* stated mourning was for three months.

Etiquette rules covered other aspects of mourning too, including communication with the family in mourning, as this 1898 article from the *Southern Echo* explained:

A card with the left hand corner folded down is left at the house of mourning, with inquiries of the servant. No effort is made to see the bereaved ones, save by intimate friends. Letters of condolence, except between close friends, are not now written. A short note of thanks is sent by the bereaved one to each donor of flowers. Cards of condolence are returned by a visiting card sent by messenger or post,

Advert for Jays, the London General Mourning Warehouse.

Lady's Own Paper – July 1854.

after a reasonable period of seclusion. Note paper and visiting cards bear a black border during the period of mourning, This varies from a mere edge line to one-sixteenth of an inch in depth according to the depth of mourning assumed. With lightened mourning, or for young girls, the line is very narrow. On black edged paper the simple monogram or address is also black.[9]

The Business of Mourning

The trappings of mourning became big business as retailers responded to the growing Victorian obsession with observing mourning etiquette, and it was an all-year-round trade. For those that couldn't afford a whole new mourning wardrobe there were plenty of places that would dye items black, from skirts and bodices to feathers. Nearly all drapers had a mourning department but specialist shops soon opened to cater for all funeral and grieving needs, and one particular London street played host to some of the biggest. In 1841 Mr W.C. Jay opened Jay's General Mourning Warehouse in three houses on Regent Street, Numbers 247, 248 and 249. Eight years later, Pugh's Mourning Warehouse opened at Number 173. Peter Robinson, who became known as Black Peter Robinson, opened his Court and General Mourning House around about this time, also on Regent Street at numbers 256, 258, 260 and 262. Finally, in 1854, the Argyll General Mourning and Mantle Warehouse opened at numbers 246 and 248.

The most well known were Jay's and Peter Robinson's, both were entirely devoted to the 'apparel and apparatus of grief'. Etiquette dictated that widows and daughters should not be seen outside before the funeral. Both companies owned black carriages with black-clad coachmen and suitably attired lady dress-fitters who were ready at a moment's notice to attend a household suddenly thrust into mourning. An advert for Jay's from 1873 reached out to potential customers: 'Sudden mourning – Messrs. Jay are always ready to travel to any part of the kingdom, free of expense to purchasers, when the emergencies of sudden or unexpected mourning require the immediate execution of mourning orders. They take with them dresses, bonnets and millinery.'[10] Similar adverts can be found for both Jay's and Peter Robinson's well into the 1890s.

Mourning dress fabrics, particularly till the Second Mourning stage were limited to bombazine and crêpe. Bombazine was made in Britain, principally in Norwich in the early nineteenth century. Quality bombazine had a silk warp and worsted weft and was twilled or corded. Black bombazine was used mainly for mourning, as was the black crêpe it was decorated with. Crêpe was a plain silk gauze stiffened with shellac and embossed by passing it over a heated revolving engraved copper cylinder, unfortunately it had a tendency to lose its texture over time. In 1887, Jay's advertised an alternative to crêpe that could be 'made up effectively into costumes for deep mourning when it is not compulsory to trim with crêpe'.[11] The material in question was Crêpe Imperial, described as 'all wool and yet looks exactly like crêpe as it has the crinkled or crimped surface which is inseparable from that fabric',[12] it was less perishable and less stretchy than silk crêpe and probably cheaper. Mourning was an expensive business and for those of the lower classes going into mourning often meant simply dyeing their usual day dress black.

A woman in mourning was allowed to wear black jewellery only. *The Queen* magazine advised that 'A few trinkets must be worn, if only to accentuate the general sombreness of the costume.'[13] There is a common misconception that all black Victorian jewellery is for mourning purposes; this is not the case because the mid- to late nineteenth century saw a general fashion for black jewellery, some of it very heavy looking. There are, however, certain symbols to look for to help identify mourning jewellery.

As with the dress fabrics worn in Full Mourning, any jewellery would have a matte-black finish, known as 'dead black'. The Victorians' love of symbolism meant certain images were associated with mourning. Crosses were an obvious symbol and were often worn as pendants. Other things to look for on brooches, pendants and other items of jewellery include oak sprays with an empty acorn cup symbolising loss; lily of the valley represented the reuniting of loved ones who have departed; weeping willows portray a deep feeling of being forsaken; forget-me-nots symbolise faithful love and memories; anchors signified hope; a hand holding a yew branch symbolised reincarnation, death and rebirth. Tiny pearls were the most common decoration on mourning pieces, they represented tears (as a contrast, they also symbolised beauty and were used extensively in wedding jewellery). Some mourning pieces, particularly those for a child or young woman, included white materials such as ivory to represent innocence.

Glossary

À disposition – horizontal border patterns emphasizing width

À la paresseuse – manner of lacing a corset which allowed the wearer to tighten her own corset

Aigrette – a long plume, especially of egret feathers

Albert crêpe – a superior quality black silk crêpe for mourning

Algerine – a twilled shot silk in either green and poppy or blue and gold

Alpaca – made from the fleece of alpacas and silk giving a soft, shiny fabric with the rustle of silk but at a much lower cost

Alpago – a stout satin delaine

Angola – made from lambs' wool

Armure – a rich silk and wool fabric with an almost invisible design

Armurette – a fancy silk and wool fabric

Balayeuse – a separate layer of flounces that would button directly to the underside of the skirt train to keep it off the ground

Ballernos – a very soft silky mohair

Balzarine – a cotton and worsted fabric similar to barège

Barathea – silk and worsted mix fabric in black, used for mourning

Barège – a semi-transparent fabric of a silk-wool mix, the silk more visible on the surface

Barège de laine – a thick woollen dimity, the right side ribbed, the other has a long soft nap

Barège de Pyrénées – barège printed with delicate foliage and bright flowers

Basque – extension to the bodice which goes below the waist

Basquin – same as the basque but cut as an integral part of the bodice

Batiste – a plain weave, fine cloth made from cotton or linen

Bavolet – on a bonnet a curtain of fabric, attached to the base of the crown which covered the neck

Bayadère silks – thick silk with a stripes of velvet woven in

Beche-cachemire – a soft, thick woollen fabric

Beige – a firm thin worsted with a smooth twill, usually coffee coloured

Bengaline – 1860s a very light mohair, plain or brocaded with very small flowers; 1880s a corded silk and wool fabric

Bergère – oval, low-crowned hat with a turned down brim

Berthe – a type of white collar made from lace or fine fabtic

Bifurcated skirt – trousers constructed to maintain the illusion of a skirt

Blonde – a type of silk lace, the name refers to the natural colour

Bombazine – twilled fabric with a silk warp and worsted weft

Bouillon – a twisted yarn fringe which generally contains threads of silver or gold

Bouracan – a ribbed poplin

Bourrette – a twilled woollen ground with multi-coloured knots and threads of spun silk on it

Bretelles – a cape like arrangement on a bodice which extended beyond the shoulders and tapered down to a V at the waist

Brocatelle – silk fabric similar to brocade but thicker and heavier, has a raised pattern

Broché – a velvet or silk with a satin design on the face

Bure – coarse woollen fabric with diagonal rib

Burnoose – a long, loose, hooded cloak

Busk – flat length of wood or metal

Byzantine granité – a dark brown wool with a few gold threads

Camayeux silk – chine silk with colour on colour

Cambric – a plain weave, light weight cloth made of linen

Cambric sarcenet – linen silk mix, plain or twilled

Cameleon – silk with a design of large bouquets on the outside and stripes inside

Camlet – resembles alpaca but slightly thicker and less glossy, a wool/ cotton mix

Carmeline – a fine cloth

Carmelite – similar to beige

Cashmere – a twilled worsted made of the wool of the Tibetan goat

Cashmere Syrien – a very soft, fine twilled cashmere without a 'wrong side'

Chalis – a mixture of silk and wool

Chased metal – metal decorated by hammering the front to raise, depress or push aside the metal without removing any from the surface

Chemisette – an under bodice of fine white fabric usually worn to supply sleeves and cover a low neckline

Chenille – French for caterpillar, a yarn with protruding fibres used for embroidery, fringing and knitted or crocheted accessories

Cheviot – a soft woollen fabric made in small checks

China crêpe – raw silk, gummed and twisted, thicker than ordinary crape

Coburg – wool and cotton twilled fabric

Coquille – French for shell, a scalloped design

Cordelière – a silk and wool mix fabric

Cording – a twisted cord of hemp or cotton inserted between two layers of fabric and stitched either side, used for stiffening

Corduroy – ribbed velvet

Coteline – striped woollen corduroy

Coutil – a twilled cotton cloth

Crape – transparent crimped silk gauze

Crêpe – see Crape

Crêpe de chine – a very soft China crêpe

Crêpeline – cheap substitute for crêpe de chine

Crepon – 1860s a China crêpe with a silky lustre and soft feel; 1880s wool, silk or mixed fabric with a silky surface resembling crêpe but thicker; 1890s a woollen fabric crêped to look puffed between stripes or squares of plain weave

Cretonne – a twilled unglazed cotton printed in colours

Crinolette – half crinoline, the mid-point between the full crinoline and the bustle

Crinoline – A stiff fabric, from the French words 'crin', horsehair, and 'lin' the linen thread it was woven with

Damask – a patterned fabric of silk or linen, the pattern appearing reversed on the back

Delaine – a high grade woollen or worsted cloth

Dimity – a stout cotton fabric, plain or twilled, with a raised pattern on one side

Drap de France – a double-twilled cashmere

Drap de velour – a thick, soft velvety cloth

Drap de Venise – a ribbed poplin

Droguet – a ribbed woollen fabric

Djedda – a poil de chevre with silk spots

Ducape – heavy corded fabric

Duchesse satin – a heavy, stiff satin

Egyptian cloth – a soft fabric of a wool and silk mix

En carré – decoration on a bodice simulating a low square neckline

Engageantes – separate white under sleeves, attaching to the inside of the bodice sleeve

En pelerine – decoration on a bodice simulating a small shoulder cape

Faille – soft, light-woven silk with a ribbed texture

Flannel – a soft woollen fabric

Foulard – light silk fabric with a soft finish and a simple twill weave

Frisette – small, curled hairpiece

Frou frou – a satin-like washing cloth

Galatea – a strong, striped cotton woven in imitation of linen

Gauging – another name for cartridge pleats

Gauze – a delicate transparent fabric of silk, or silk and flax, or cotton

Genappe cloth – fabric of wool and cotton striped in two shades of the same colour

Genoa velvet – a fabric with a satin ground and arabesque figures in velvet

Gigot – another term for the leg-of-mutton sleeve

Gimp – a twisted silk, worsted or cotton cord

Gingham – cotton or linen checked cloth

Glacé – fabric with a lustrous quality

Goaly – a kind of éry silk with a texture like fine canvas

Gores – triangular pieces of fabric used to give extra fullness

Grelots – ball fringing

Grenadine – an open silk, or silk and wool, gauze

Gros or Gros Grain – a stout corded silk, the cord running across rather than vertically

Gros de Naples – a corded Italian silk

Gros de Rome – a crinkled silk between a China crêpe and a foulard

Gros de Tours – a rich corded silk

Holland – plain woven linen

Hopsack – fabric with a basket type weave

Horsehair – stiff, open weave fabric

Imperial velvet – fabric composed of alternate stripes of corded silk and velvet, the latter double the width of the former

Jacconet – a thin cotton, between muslin and cambric, similar to nainsook.

Japanese pongee – a silk of the same texture as a crêpe but with a smooth surface

Japanese silk – a silk fabric resembling alpaca

Knickerbocker – a thick, coarse woollen fabric, self coloured or speckled

Laine foulard – a silk and wool washing silk

Leno – a transparent muslin like fabric of linen thread

Levantine – a rich faced, stout, twilled silk

Limousine – a thick, hairy, rough wool

Linsey – a coarse fabric of wool and flax

Longcloth – plain cotton cloth

Macarons – a row of rosettes or large buttons from neck to hem

Madras – type of muslin with a transparent ground with a pattern of thick soft thread darned upon it

Mancheron – an ornamental trimming on the upper part of the sleeve

Mantle – A generic term for a loose outer garment, wrap or cape, usually without sleeves

Mariposa – a washing sateen with stripes alternately plain and spotted

Matelassé – a form of heavy, brocaded silk woven to resemble quilting

Melton – thick woollen cloth which has been 'fulled' to give it a felt like smooth surface, it is napped and very closely sheared

Merino – a thin woollen, or wool and silk mix, twilled cloth made from the wool of the merino sheep

Merino, satin – fabric where the right side is finer and more silky than cashmere, the wrong side resembles plush

Mikado – imitation Japanese silk

Mohair – fabric made from the hair of the angora goat, woven with silk, wool or cotton

Moiré – fabric with a watered appearance, mainly silk

Mousseline de laine – a fine light woollen cloth with a muslin-like texture

Muslin – a fine, semi-transparent cotton

Nainsook – a delicate muslin

Nankin – a pale yellow cotton cloth from China

Natté – a firm, substantial silk woven to resemble cane-plaiting

Neigeuse – speckled or flecked woollens

Nun's veiling – a thin woollen barège like a voile

Organdy – a plain weave stiff cotton

Orleans cloth – similar to an un-twilled Coburg, the warp of thin cotton, the weft of worsted

Ottoman silk – loosely applied to all silks with a horizontal thick cord and two or three cords between

Ottoman velvet – a velvet with coloured pattens brocaded over it

Parmatta – a kind of bombazine, the weft is of worsted, the warp of cotton

Pardessus – generic term for a half- or three quarter-length outer garment shaped at the waist with a pelerine

Passementerie – a collective name given to trimmings made from braid, gold or silver cord, beads etc

Pekin – generic term for striped silk

Pekin Victoria – a silk with a satiné ground, shot in white and cherry or blue, with patterns in white

Pelerine – a short cape with pointed ends at the centre front

Pelisse – an outer garment, type of mantle

Percale – a fine, slightly glazed calico with a small printed design

Percaline – fabric between gingham and muslin, striped or quadrilled and printed with flowers

Pinking/Pinked – cutting fabric edges in a zigzag pattern to reduce fraying

Plaid – chequered or tartan twilled cloth

Plastron – a front panel in a bodice, often pleated vertically or puffed out

Plush – a shaggy, hairy silk or cotton velvet with a long, soft nap

Poil de chevre – fabric of goats hair with a shiny satin like surface

Pompadour chiné – a woollen twilled fabric with a small chiné pattern and minute horizontal stripes

Pompadour duchesse – a satin with broad stripes divided by other stripes sprinkled with tiny flowers

Pompadour silk – silk with a black background and a highly raised pattern in detached sprigs, in lemon, rose and green

Poplin – a kind of rep made from a silk warp and wool or worsted weft, having a fine corded surface

Poplinette – made with a glazed thread and silk

Poplin lama – similar to mousseline de laine but softer and thicker

Poult de soie – high quality corded silk; 1860s a mixture of silk and alpaca with a shiny surface

Quadrilled (fabric) – with a design of squares

Radzimir – a deep black silk used for mourning

Rep – fabric of silk, silk and wool, or wool only, woven in fine cords or ribs across the width

Rep bluets – a dark blue silk pattern with cornflowers in black satin

Revers – a turned-back edge revealing the underside, especially at the lapel.

Revers de pelerine – flat pleats converging from shoulder to waist down the bodice in a deep V

Ruching – a gathered overlay

Sarsenet – a thin silk, plain or twilled

Sateen – a cotton fabric with a satin face

Satin – a silk twill, glossy on the surface, dull on the back

Satin de chine – a satin of silk and worsted

Satin foullards – a silk fabric with wither spots or stripes

Satin jean – a finely twilled cotton with a satin gloss

Satin merveilleux – a soft twilled satin with a brighter face and duller back

Satin Turc – a soft, vibrant woollen fabric

Saxony cloth – a dark printed woollen material

Serge – a loosely woven, twilled fabric

Serge royale – fabric of flax and wool with a bright, silky appearance

Shantung pongee – an undyed, thin, soft, China silk

Shot – woven from warp and weft yarn of two or more colours producing an iridescent appearance

Sicilienne – a fine quality poplin with a silk warp and cashmere wool weft

Silesia – a fine brown glazed linen, used for lining

Silk, Chiné – silk fabric with a pattern that appears to have 'run'

Silk, figured – having a pattern woven into it

Silk, glacé – a plain lustrous silk

Silk, Ottoman – silk with a pronounced ribbed or corded effect

Silk, shot – woven from warp and weft yarn of two or more colours producing an iridescent appearance

Silk, Tussore – soft raw silk from India

Soufflets – pleated fans inserted into the lower part of a skirt to increase the width of the hem

Soutache – a narrow, flat braid

Soyeux linsey – a light colourful woollen poplin

Stockinette – a machine made knitted fabric, usually tubular

Sultane – a fabric of silk and mohair in alternate stripes of clear or satin

Surah – a bright, soft Indian silk, twilled on both sides, more substantial than foullard

Swiss Waist – a boned double pointed 'belt' worn over the blouse and skirt

Taffeta – a crisp, smooth plain woven fabric made from silk

Tamative – a light fabric resembling grenadine but thicker

Tarlatan – a much stiffened, thin, gauze-like fabric

Tattersall – a general name for fabric with small regularly spaced plaids or checks

Tatting – a method of making lace using a small shuttle and a series of knots and loops

Terry velvet – a silk fabric with a fine corded surface, no resemblance to velvet.

Thibet – soft thick, flannel like cloth with the long hair of a goat on the surface

Tripoline – a twilled satin Turc

Tulle – a fine silk net

Turin velvet – a fabric of silk and wool imitating terry

Tussore – soft raw silk from India

Twill – fabric weave that produces a diagonal rib

Umritza – a type of cashmere introduced by Liberty's

Valencia – cloth used for riding habits

Velours de laine – velvet stripes or checks on a woollen ground

Velour frisé – a curled, rich silk plush

Veloutine – corded merino wool fabric

Velveteen – imitation silk velvet, silk pile on a cotton back

Velvet Impératrice – a dark terry velvet

Vicuna – a very soft woollen fabric

Vigogne – a neutral-coloured all-wool cloth

Winsey – a cotton- and wool-mix fabric resembling linsey

Zephyr – a light, fine, silky gingham

Notes

Introduction

1. Oddey, S.A. and H. *Critical Review, or Annals of Literature* (London 1808)
2. John Bell died in 1845 but the magazine was carried on by his son John Browne Bell
3. *Glasgow Herald*, 19 September 1889

Chapter 1

1. *Ladies Pocket Magazine*, May 1837
2. *World of Fashion*, August 1839
3. *The Globe*, 31 August 1839
4. *The Globe,* 31 August 1839
5. *The Monmouthshire Merlin*, 7 September 1839
6. Ibid
7. *The Tipperary Free Press*, 15 February 1840
8. *The World of Fashion & Monthly Magazine of the Courts of London & Paris*, February 1841
9. *The Leeds Intelligencer*, 4 April 1840
10. *The Handbook of the Toilette*, 1841
11. *The Leeds Intelligencer*, 4 July 1840
12. Anon, *The Handbook of the Toilette* (London 1841)
13. Ibid
14. *Anon, The Handbook of the Toilette* (London 1839)
15. *The Leeds Intelligencer*, 4 July 1840
16. *The Bristol Mercury*, 2 May 1840
17. Howell, Mrs M.J., *Handbook of Millinery* (London 1847)
18. Ibid
19. Anon, *The Handbook of the Toilette* (London 1841)
20. Ibid
21. Ibid
22. *Illustrated London News*, 20 May 1843
23. *Stamford Mercury*, 13 November 1840
24. *The World of Fashion*, February 1841

Chapter 2

1. *Illustrated London News*, 26 September 1857
2. *The World of Fashion*, 1853

3. *Ladies Treasury*, 1858
4. *Lady's Own Paper*, 5 June 1858
5. *Newcastle Journal*, 20 July 1850
6. Reports by the Juries on the Subjects in the Thirty Classes into which the Exhibition was Divided, 1852
7. Habits of Good Society (Anon), 1855
8. Ibid
9. Ibid
10. *Illustrated London News* 11 October 1851
11. Ibid
12. *Bolton Chronicle*, 1 November 1851
13. *Illustrated London News* 27 September 1851
14. Ibid
15. Merrifield,Mrs, *Dress as a Fine Art*, 1854
16. *The World of Fashion*, 1 January 1852

Chapter 3
1. *The English Woman's Domestic Magazine*, 1 February 1869
2. *Wells Journal*, 31 January 1863
3. *Lancaster Guardian*, 23 October 1862
4. *Monmouthshire Beacon*, 19 December 1863
5. *Glasgow Herald*, 9 January 1862
6. *The Leicester Journal*, 12 February 1864
7. *Hereford Times*, 26 January 1861
8. *Newcastle Journal*, 20 October 1863
9. Lord, William Barry, *The Corset & the Crinoline – a Book of Modes and Costumes from Remote Periods to the Present Time* (London 1868)
10. *The Englishwoman's Domestic Magazine*, 1866
11. *The Times*, 15 December 1866

Chapter 4
1. *Dundee Courier*, 3 January 1873
2. *South London Press*, 13 November 1869
3. *Daily Review*, 3 January 1880
4. *Daily Review* 3 January 1880
5. *Sylvia's Home Journal*, 1877
6. *Ladies Treasury*, 1876
7. *The Carmarthen Journal*, 7 March 1879
8. *Bristol Daily Post*, 10 March 1863
9. *The Paisley Herald*, 11 December 1869
10. *The Cheltenham Mercury*, 15 January 1870
11. *Leicester Chronicle*, 8 December 1877
12. *Cheltenham Chronicle* 4 February 1879
13. Ibid

14. *Cheltenham Chronicle* 4 February 1879
15. *Monmouthshire Merlin* 7 June 1878
16. *Leicester Chronicle* 5 October 1878
17. *Southern Reporter* 30 March 1876
18. *Bedfordshire Mercury* 4 January 1879
19. Price, Julius Mendes *Dame Fashion: Paris – London 1786–1912* (London 1913)
20. Greenwood, James *In Strange Company, Being the Experiences of a Roving Correspondent* (London1874)
21. Ibid

Chapter 5
1. *The Young Ladies Journal*, January 1884
2. Ballin, Miss Ada S. *The Science of Dress in Theory & Practice*, 1885
3. Ibid
4. Ibid
5. Ibid
6. Ibid
7. Ibid
8. *The Girls Own Paper,* 1884
9. Ibid
10. Ballin, Miss Ada S. *The Science of Dress in Theory and Practice* (London 1885)
11. Adburgham, Alison *Shops and Shopping 1800–1914* (London 1981)
12. *Illustrated London News*, 18 June 1887
13. *London Evening Standard*, 17 May 1881
14. Trade card for Madame Marie Fontaine's Bosom Beautifier c.1882
15. *The Young Ladies Journal*, 1884
16. *The Queen*, 10 September 1887
17. *The Queen*, 10 September 1887
18. Ibid
19. *The Young Ladies Journal*, 1884
20. Jaeger, Dr Guatav, *Dr Jaeger's Sanitary Woolen System* (London 1884)
21. Jaeger, Dr Guatav, *Dr Jaeger's Sanitary Woolen System* (London 1884)
22. *Dundee Evening Telegraph*, 10 April 1882
23. *Aberdeen Evening Express*, 12 February 1887
24. Ibid
25. Ibid
26. *Rational Dress Society Gazette*, January 1889
27. *Aberdeen Evening News*, February 1887
28. Ballin, Miss Ada S. *The Science of Dress* (London 1885)

Chapter 6
1. *The Woman at Home* Vol, 4 1895
2. *The Woman at Home*, 1894

3. *The Woman at Home*, 1896
4. Ibid
5. Ibid
6. *Bicycling News*, 1893
7. *The Woman at Home* Volume 4, 1895
8. *Yorkshire Evening Post* 15 February 1896
9. *Journal of the Kew Guild*, 1896
10. Ibid
11. *The Woman at Home*, 1896
12. *The Woman at Home*, 1894
13. *Gentlewoman Magazine*, August 1899
14. Warren, Philip and Nicol, Sarah *Foundations of Fashion: The Symington Corsetry Collection 1860–1890* (Leicester 2013)
15. *The Queen*, 25 November 1893.
16. *The Queen*, 5 August 1899
17. *The Queen*, 14 April 1894
18. *The Woman at Home*, 1894
19. *The Woman at Home*, 1896
20. *The Woman at Home*, 1896
21. *The Woman at Home*, 1894
22. *Doughty, R.W., Feather Fashions and Bird Preservation: a Study in Nature Protection, (California 1975)*
23. Moore-Colyer, R.J. *Feathered Women and Persecuted Birds* (Cambridge 2000)
24. *The Woman at Home*, 1896

Chapter 8
1. *Leicester Chronicle*, 24 June 1837
2. *Cambridge Chronicle*, 1 July 1837
3. *The Sun* 6 December 1861
4. *Northampton Mercury*, 4 January 1862
5. Ibid
6. See Curl, James Stevens *The Victorian Celebration of Death* (Stroud 2004)
7. Beeton, Isabella *Beeton's Housewife's Treasury of Domestic Information* (London 1879)
8. *The Queen*, 24 February 1900
9. *Southern Echo*, 17 January 1898
10. *Globe*, 10 June 1873
11. *The Queen*, 8 October 1887
12. Ibid
13. *The Queen*, 1892

Select Bibliography

Adburgham, Alison, *Shops and Shopping*, (London, 1964)

Anon, *Habits of Good Society,* (1855)

Ashelford Jane, *The Art of Dress – Clothes and Society 1500–1914*, (London, 2000)

Ballin, Ada S., *The Science of Dress in Theory and Practice*, (London, 1885)

Cunnington, C. Willett, *English Women's Clothing in the Nineteenth Century* (New York, 1990)

Doughty, Robin W., *Feathered Fashions and Bird Preservation: A Study in Nature Protection*, (University of California Press, 1975)

Gernsheim, Alison., *Victorian and Edwardian Fashion: A Photographic Survey,* (New York, 1981)

Ginsberg, Madeleine., *Victorian Dress in Photographs*, (London 1988)

Greenwood, James., *In Strange company, Being the Experiences of a Roving Correspondent*, (London, 1883)

Howell, Mary J., *The Handbook of Millinery*, (London,1847)

Jaeger, Dr G., *Dr Jaegers Sanitary Woollen System,* (London 1884)

Johnston, Lucy., *Nineteenth Century Fashion in Detail,* (London, 2006)

Lord, William Barry, *The Corset and the Crinoline: A Book of Modes and Costumes from Remote Periods to the Present Time*, (London, 1868)

Lynn, Eleri, *Underwear Fashion in Detail*, (London, 2010)

Merrifield, Nary, *Dress as a Fine Art*, (Boston, 1854)

Moore-Colyer, R.J., *Feathered Women and Persecuted Birds: The Struggle Against the Plumage Trade* c.1860–1922, (Cambridge University Press, 2000)

Pitcher, Izabella, *The Victorian Dressmaker*, (2018)

Price, J.M., *Dame Fashion: Paris – London (1786–1912)*, (London, 1913)

Reports by the Juries on the Subjects in the Thirty Classes into which the Exhibition is Divided (London, 1852)

The Handbook of the Toilette, (London, 1841)

Newspapers, Magazines and Journals

Aberdeen Evening Express

Bedfordshire Mercury

Bicycling News

Bolton Chronicle

Bristol Daily Post

Bristol mercury, The

Cambridge Chronicle and Journal

Carmarthen Journal, The

Cheltenham Chronicle, The

Cheltenham Mercury, The

Daily Review (Edinburgh)

Dundee Courier

Dundee Evening telegraph

English Woman's Domestic Magazine, The

Gentlewoman Magazine

Girls Own Paper, The

Globe, The

Glasgow Herald

Hereford Times

Illustrated London News, The

Journal of the Kew Guild, The
Ladies' Treasury
Lady's Own Paper
Lancaster Guardian
Leeds Intelligencer, The
Leicester Chronicle
Leicester Journal, The
London Evening Standard
Monmouthshire Beacon
Monmouthshire merlin, The
Newcastle Journal
Northampton Mercury
Paisley Herald, The
Queen, The
Rational Dress Society Gazette

Southern Echo
Southern Reporter
South London Chronicle
South London Press
Stanford Mercury
Sun
Sylvia's Home Journal
Times, The
Wells Journal
Woman at Home, The
World of Fashion and Continental Feulletons, The
Yorkshire Evening Post
Young Ladies Journal, The

Index